Just Like Mima's

THE HEART
BEHIND THE
CUBAN RECIPES
WE ALL LOVE

BY MARILYN MARRERO

Illustrations by Janelle Audrey Marrero
Photography by Julianna Beatriz Marrero

Dedicated to:

Our *Familión* [*fah-mee-lee-ohn*]: A multi-generational, affectionate, hilarious, good-food-loving, fun bunch that loves to make beautiful memories together. We are truly blessed to be a part of this one-of-a-kind family.

This has been a labor of love in honor and appreciation of our beloved matriarch, Mima. A simple, familiar, endearing name that evokes so much admiration – not just from our *Familión,* but from anyone who knows her.

Among all our unique experiences, these two constants have been there for all of us: Mima's unconditional love and unrivaled cooking.

What greater compliment than to hear
that our hearts are courageous…
that our homes are welcoming…
or that the aroma of something
we've cooked is mouthwatering…
Just Like Mima's?

I am so excited to share her story and her recipes with you!

Contents:

INTRODUCTION:
Y Llegaron 6... (And They Were Once Just 6...)

The Heart

40 years ago, our family emigrated from Cuba to the United States during the Mariel Boatlift of 1980. (Lots more on that later.)

Back then, it was just my grandparents – Mima and Pipo – and their four kids – Tere, Toti, Cary and Papito. I was born the following year: Mima and Pipo's first granddaughter and the first Cuban-American in the family.

I had no concept of what that meant, of course, until I was much older.

As the only kid in the family for five years – while they all adjusted to a new language, new foods, new friends and new customs – I happily ate (Mima's food and fast food), danced (salsa and pop), laughed and dreamed (in Spanish and English). I was surrounded by the love of my parents *and* my extended family.

This is an aspect of my life that I often look back on with great fondness. I got to spend a lot of time with my grandparents, something many latchkey kids in my generation didn't experience. I know our *"Familión"* – as we affectionately call our big family – has helped shape me into the person I am today.

Mima, in particular, is there in all my most significant memories.

Mima pulled out my loose teeth. And in case you're wondering, yes, she did have jewelry made with some of them.

She made me chicken soup and comforted me whenever I was sick.

Marilyn Marrero, Cruz María Herrera (Mima) and Eusebio Herrera (Pipo).

My hair grew curly and unmanageable as I got older, so Mima splurged and got a pricey set of hair care products she'd seen on TV to help me out. Unfortunately, it didn't work quite as well as the commercials promised.

I did my homework on her kitchen table with the sound of *el noticiero* (evening news) in the background, while something tasty cooked on her stove.

Whenever I got frustrated with a homework assignment, she would push me to keep going. "*No te tupas.* (Don't let yourself get stuck.) Try another way."

Among a myriad of other things, she taught me how to sit up straight, sweep the floor, shop the specials, thread a needle and stitch, and balance a checkbook.

She listened with compassion when I shared my dreams, fears, and difficult decisions – and then spoke priceless words of encouragement and wisdom.

Now that I have a family of my own, she is a part of those memories, too.

On our wedding day, we took a picture looking out the back window of the car after the ceremony, just like my favorite photo from her wedding.

Several others in our *Familión* have also done this, which has become a really sweet way to honor Mima and Pipo.

Left to right: Eusebio (Pipo) and Cruz María Herrera (Mima) – 1960; Jonathan and Marilyn Marrero – 2005; Dayana and Kevin Herrera – 2013; Robert and Maggie Cruz ("Baby" Maggie) – 2019.

Janelle Audrey Marrero, Cruz María Herrera (Mima) and Julianna Beatriz Marrero.

She was there when my first ultrasound revealed that my husband and I were having twins, and ecstatically shouted, *"¡Yo lo sabía!"* (I knew it!) I saw her delight in being promoted to great-grandmother, lovingly holding my teeny preemie daughters, Janelle and Julianna, one in each arm.

When Julianna's reflux was so bad that she wasn't gaining weight, Mima started feeding her baby cereal, even though she was technically too young for solid food. That quickly put an end to what the doctors called "failure to thrive."

She pulled Janelle's first loose tooth out. She got the girls' first bikes. She "practiced her English" as they giggled uncontrollably. She taught them how to untangle their hair at bedtime, and how to properly dab their mouths with a napkin at the dinner table. She has spent weeks at a time taking care of them during breaks from school, taking turns sleeping with one of them each night.

My girls *love* Mima. They love spending time with her, as much as I always have.

A few years ago, newly-married Jonathan and I moved from Miami, where we both grew up, to Cary, North Carolina... back to Miami again... and finally, back to Cary again with our two girls. (That's a long story for some other time.)

One of the hardest things about leaving, for me, was leaving Mima.

Despite my reluctance to tell her, each time she responded with reassurance and love. She understood like no one else the feelings of leaving home, comfort, familiarity and loved ones behind. She has taken multiple steps into the unknown, with unwavering faith, wherever God has called her.

We live more than 800 miles from my family, so I treasure the time we do get to spend together. But since that doesn't happen as a part of our everyday lives, I really want my girls to know our family and our story. I want them to be able to cook one of their favorite dishes someday, and tell their kids, "This is how Mima made it." That's how this idea began to take shape.

And it's not just for my girls. Mima and Pipo's children all have kids, sons- and daughters-in-laws, step-kids and grandkids of their own. Mima now has more than 10 great-grandkids, ranging from newborn to age 11!

When I was younger, I remember Pipo's brother, Ernesto, looking around during family gatherings and chuckling, "*Y llegaron 6...*" (And they were once just 6...) It *is* amazing to see how much our family tree has grown. Each of us – bigger branches or itty bitty leaves on the tree – has special memories, physical and personality traits, values and dreams that come from those strong roots.

The Recipes

I love to cook. I know that's something I learned from Mima. The secret ingredient in every dish, she always says, is a whole lot of love.

So over the past couple of years, whenever Mima would come to visit us in North Carolina, I would ask her to teach me. We shopped together, sometimes stopping at multiple grocery stores just to find one ingredient. (It's not always easy to find plantains outside of cities with big Cuban communities, like Miami.)

I recorded her recipes, which usually do not include measurements, or specific temperature settings, or exact cooking times. After she went back home, I tried to make them on my own. I called her and asked more questions.

And on, and on... Until I was finally able to write the recipes out in a way that would make sense to others. To share them with you!

But before we get to the recipes, let's get back to the heart.

Whether you are a member of our *Familión*, a neighbor or friend interested in one of Mima's recipes, or even if you'd never heard of Mima before someone handed you this book... You need to hear Mima's story.

Because it's pretty remarkable. Just like Mima.

PART ONE – MIMA'S STORY:
No Me Puedo Quejar (I Can't Complain)

Photo courtesy of Karina Gudiel.

"I will always be amazed at Mima's desire and hard work to better her life and her family's. Ever since she was a little girl, big and beautiful dreams were within her."

María Teresa Suarez (Tere) – daughter

Chapter 1:
Hope-Filled Dreams

Those of us who have never been to Cuba can almost instinctively picture it. The beautiful beaches... The charming Spanish colonial architecture... The lively music... The vibrant dishes... The colorful vintage cars.

We have seen Cuba, with all its glamour and allure, on TV and in movies over the years.

Cuban *guajiros* (country people) are no less beautiful, charming, lively, vibrant or colorful. But the daily difficulties and inequalities these Cubans have experienced in the rural areas are not quite as glamorous or alluring.

In the 1930s, many of these families lived in extreme poverty, lacked access to education and medical care, and experienced hunger and malnourishment. This is the time and place in which Cruz María Espinosa Garcés – known to most of us as Mima – was born on May 25, 1936.

84 years later, Mima and I sit and talk while sipping our coffees on a bright summer morning. We've done this many times before. But I've come prepared this time, with a list of questions on my laptop, and my cellphone ready to record her bubbling laughter and soothing voice as we chat.

She tells me stories I've heard dozens of times over the years. A few I'd never fully understood until now. And others I'd not heard before at all.

Let's go back to 1936 and start at the beginning...

Uvaldo Espinosa (Valdo) and Clara Aurora Garcés (Aurora).

Mima was the firstborn of Clara Aurora Garcés (daughter of Josefa and Guillermo Garcés) and Uvaldo Espinosa (son of Victoriana and Atilano Espinosa).

She was born in San Germán, part of the eastern province of Holguín, Cuba. Her mother gave birth at home with the help of a midwife, since there were no hospitals nearby.

She was named Cruz after her father's sister, and because she was born with dark black hair and tan skin, her father gave her the nickname "Mulata." The name just stuck, and Mima says that many people in her neighborhood never actually knew her real name.

Her mother, who was known as Aurora, and her father, who was known as Valdo, were very young. They had only been married for a short time when Mima was born. Aurora and Valdo were both originally from Velasco (also in Holguín), but had moved to San Germán in search of better opportunities.

They lived in a *caserío* (housing project) near the sugar processing factory, where her father worked. The neighborhood they lived in was called Gutiérrez. Mima recalls hearing a siren coming from the factory, around 1 a.m. every night, and the constant sounds of the train, "*Chaca-chaca, chaca-chaca.*"

Aurora and Valdo went on to have nine more children after Mima. In fact, when the youngest was born, Mima was already 20 years old! Her nine younger siblings, in order of birth, are: Emelina, Elda, Juan, Rey, Aida, Aurora (Aurorita), Atilano (Nan), Uvaldo (Uvaldito), and Renán.

Because Mima was the oldest child, her siblings always looked up to her and respected her a lot.

As she cared for them, she developed many attributes – among these, sacrificial love, patience, compassion, and empathy – for which she is still well known today.

Uvaldito died when he was 12 years old, and Aurorita died by suicide as an adult, but the others are still living in Cuba, where Mima is still affectionately known as "Mulata" or "Muli" by all of them.

After a few years in San Germán, Mima's parents decided to move to Santa Cruz (also in Holguín), where her two youngest siblings were born. Her father was looking for land to farm, and better working conditions.

"Things only got worse from there on out, but they tried..." she says.

Her parents' house had a roof made of dried palm fronds, with walls of *yagua* (palm tree leaves), and a compacted dirt floor. In the back of the house, there was a hangover roof that covered a small, wood-burning stove. There was a small living room in the center of the house, with one bedroom on either side.

The children all slept in one room together; Aurora and Valdo slept in the other. Only the youngest child at the time would be allowed to sleep with them.

This is the same house Mima would later return to visit with her own kids, and where her mother and father stayed until they were too old to live on their own. They later moved in with her brother, Juan.

I glance around and realize the living room we're sitting in is probably the size of the entire house they all lived in for all those years.

We're spending a few days at a beach rental in Naples, Florida with my parents, my sister, and each of our families. There are 11 of us here now, for the next four days. There were 12 of them there, then...

Raising 10 children in the 1940s, in a one-income household, within a very rural area of Cuba, was as challenging as you might imagine.

Mima says her father made the equivalent of $1.50 a day, and his earnings only covered the bare basics for food: rice and oil.

One day, there was no food to eat, and Mima stumbled upon a nest with some eggs in it. She snatched them up and ran home, eager to show her mother.

"I was so excited, and running so fast, that I tripped over my own two feet. Because I didn't want to let go of the eggs, so they wouldn't break, I got all scraped up when I hit the floor. But the eggs were fine! I hid all my injuries from my mother until after my father had eaten."

Mima says her mother often pointed out how hard her father worked, day after day, under the beating sun. Physical labor was especially difficult for him, because he'd suffered from severe asthma since birth.

"The best, most nutritious food was always set aside for him," she says.

Both of Mima's grandfathers died at a young age, but she did get to spend time with her grandmothers. She was very close to her maternal grandmother, Chefa, who lived to be 97 years old. Mima says she was very kind and loving.

Mima remembers wanting to nap with Chefa, but Chefa would tell her that little kids should not sleep with old people. So once Chefa was asleep, Mima would sneak into the bed and snuggle with her.

"It's so sweet to dream wrapped up in the warm embrace of a loving grandmother," she says with a smile. I couldn't agree more.

"I love Mima's warm, soft hands! They are comforting in any situation."
Maggie Cruz ("Baby" Maggie) – granddaughter

One of Mima's aunts, who was named América, was also very special to her. Even though she lived in Velasco, Mima says they would sometimes take the train from San Germán to visit her.

"América spoiled me because I was her first niece. She was very kind to all my children later on, too," she says.

Mima says that as a child, she could never remember a time when her mother was not pregnant or nursing a newborn. She recalls seeing her struggle, knowing she was weak and tired, and wanting to help however she could.

Once, when her mother was too nauseous to cook – she was pregnant once again – Mima decided to help by making something for her father to eat.

"But the oil I was frying with was too hot, so it splattered and filled my face with red dots. My mother got very upset and scolded me for meddling," she says.

Mima had one dress that she couldn't ever wear, because it was only for special occasions, which never seemed to come around. When she finally got permission to wear it, she asked her father to help her fasten the back.

"He angrily said to take it off, because it looked like my butt was hanging out! It was already too small," she says.

Mima didn't go to school past the first grade, even though she enjoyed going, when she could. She says she was overcome with sadness whenever she saw her siblings and other neighborhood kids walking to school. Her parents didn't say she *couldn't* go, but as the oldest, she had to help with a lot of the chores around the house. Everything had to be done before she could leave for school.

One morning, she says, she was determined to go.

"I finished all my housework early. I was so eager to get there that I made it all the way to the school before I realized I hadn't washed up. My arms were dirty, all the way up to my elbows. I was so embarrassed that I left," she says.

At her school, the teachers would put up the best drawings on the board each week. Mima says she arrived early one Friday, and immediately saw they had put up her drawing of a fish! "I was so happy! That's why every time I have a paper and pencil in my hand, I draw a fish," she says, demonstrating for me.

As she got older, Mima says she realized that if she worked instead of going to school, she could help provide for her family's needs. "I saw my younger siblings almost as my own kids. I wanted something better for all of them."

"Mima is naturally maternal, loving and kind to everyone. We have been blessed to have such an exemplary mother, and grandmother to our kids."
María Caridad García (Cary) – daughter

I start to wonder what else she liked to do as a child, and I ask her. She thinks quietly for a while before answering, "Oh, I don't know. I guess I never had enough free time to think about that."

At the age of 14, Mima started working in other homes, washing and ironing clothes for other families in her neighborhood. Eventually, she began working at homes in other areas of Holguín. Some of her sisters were old enough to help around the house by then, and her brothers helped her father in the fields.

With the money she made, she was able to buy new shoes for herself and her siblings, for the first time. She also bought some fabric and made a dress for herself. "Everyone had something to say about how beautiful and fashionable my dress was," she says.

Whether it involved making extra money or not, Mima says she always desired to help others. Whenever someone in her extended family was sick, or had a new baby, she would go stay with them for a few weeks.

She remembers, "Sometimes I helped take care of their kids. Other times I cleaned or cooked. People often say, 'I wish I had more money so I could help others.' But there's always something you can do to help, and that was my way. Even now that I'm old, when I go back to visit, they remember and still thank me. That's my reward."

"Two things I've learned from Mima – not because she says them, but because she does them – are the importance of working hard, and the concept of thinking of others first."
Emmanuel Matos (Manny) – grandson

Captivating Eyes

Around the age of 14, Mima says, she began to notice that she had a unibrow. "I had this cousin named Sebastián, and he had a very thick unibrow, and – poor thing – he was so ugly. People sometimes teased me and told me I looked like Sebastián. I would cry and beg my mother to help me pluck my eyebrows."

But her mother said she was still too young for that. Not being one to wait around for help, Mima found a razor and did it herself. She was so nervous that she accidentally took about half of her eyebrow out!

She tells me bashfully, her cheeks almost matching her bright coral shirt, as if it had just happened.

"I kept looking away and trying to hide my face from my mother, so she wouldn't notice. But, of course, she did. And she was so mad! It felt like an eternity waiting for that eyebrow to grow back. But when it finally did, and we shaped them correctly, I looked totally different!"

"You know, I had an *enamorado* (admirer) when I was young who said he'd seen many beautiful women, but none had eyes like mine," she adds.

I have always loved the kindness and patience in Mima's beautiful eyes.

Today, there is an extra sparkle in her eyes, as she revels in the opportunity to share these memories.

Mima says her family didn't really celebrate holidays or birthdays when she was young. One year, her brothers and some neighborhood friends who had a guitar surprised her with a serenade for her birthday.

She says with amusement, "They were pretty scared of my father, thinking he might run them off. But he was actually delighted to hear the music."

For *Noche Buena* (December 24), they would gather and eat with extended family, but it was not considered a religious celebration.

"It wasn't about the true meaning of Christmas or Jesus' birth for us," she says. "We didn't really talk about anything like that."

Some other families in their neighborhood celebrated *Día de Reyes* (Three Kings' Day), and she never understood why her family didn't.

"I finally worked up the nerve to ask my mother, 'Why do all the other kids in the neighborhood receive toys from the *Reyes* (Wise Men) when they behave well?' My mother quietly thought for a while before explaining that the '*Reyes*' were actually their parents, and that not all families could afford to buy gifts."

"Knowing the truth made me feel so much better. All those years I thought maybe it was because I wasn't being good enough," she says.

There was no church near their house, so Mima and her family didn't attend church or talk about God very much. "They baptized us, because that was the traditional thing to do, but not because of our faith. Everyone did it."

"There was a traveling priest who would come by the neighborhood and collect the names of all the children who needed to be baptized. Then he would come back on the appointed day and do it all at once," she says.

There was a blend of tradition, spiritualism, religion and superstition all mixed into her upbringing.

She recounts a story I'd never heard before – apparently triggered by the intense thunderstorm she and my sister had just experienced on the way to the beach house the night before.

Mima says one afternoon, Chefa, one of her aunts, and her paternal grandmother (who was known as Tana) were terrified of a dark storm cloud they could see approaching.

"They all ran outside and started praying, making the sign of the cross and saying, '*Reprende, Dios mío.*' (Rebuke this storm, my God.) One was crying out to 'Jesus the Nazarene,' another brought out a handful of ashes and started anointing their foreheads in the shape of a cross, and another was making the sign of the cross with a machete."

She can barely get the words out because she is laughing so much. To say her laughter is contagious is an understatement.

"I can laugh about it now, telling you the story. But you have no idea how much it terrified me and my younger siblings to see them acting like that and wondering if the world was about to end," she says.

"One of the things that I love most about Mima is her laugh."
Emmanuel Matos (Manny) – grandson

Chapter 2:
Admirable Work Ethic

By the time she was 17, Mima took a more permanent job with the Suegro family in Holguín. The couple ran a photography studio, and the wife (Josefa) was also studying to be a teacher. Mima took care of their newborn son, Eddy, whenever Josefa had to go to the university in Havana for her exams.

After Josefa finished her exams, she recommended Mima to one of her uncles in Holguín, and they hired her.

Eulogio and Francisca Franco were from Spain. Francisca was going to have surgery, so they needed someone to help around the house temporarily. They had two older kids, including a daughter who was almost Mima's age.

Mima says she did practically everything there, but they saw how hard she worked, and they were all very good to her. "They were very caring and generous, telling me, 'People who work hard need to eat well.'"

"Mima is a fighter. She's not afraid of working hard. I think in some ways my personality is like hers. I am hard-working, maternal, and I like to help others. But the other parts of my personality are more like Pipo's!"
María Caridad García (Cary) – daughter

Mima says the Francos' home is where she really learned to cook well.

When she was younger, she'd helped her mother cook, but there wasn't really any time for teaching or recipes. She admits that her mother wasn't the best cook, either.

"We improvised and did what we could with the little we had," she says.

She recalls a time when, after getting a haircut, she contemplated buying herself a soda with the 25 cents she had left. Instead, she decided to buy some ground beef and noodles. When she got home, she and her mother boiled some vegetables and made a hearty stew for the whole family.

"Instead of just me enjoying the soda, we all ate."

"My grandmother, Chefa, was there that day. She always talked about how delicious that stew was. That experience also taught me the significance of just *one* memorable meal shared with love," she says.

*"I'm not just saying this because she's my mom. The reality is I've never
met anyone like Mima. She is loving, caring, generous, unselfish – she
would give up anything, not just for her family, but for anyone in need –
always putting others before herself."*
María Teresa Suarez (Tere) – daughter

"Once I started working at other houses, where they had better-equipped
kitchens, full refrigerators, and all kinds of supplies, it was like a school for me.
I really grew to enjoy cooking. What might seem like a punishment to some –
being a household servant – was something I was thankful for," she recalls.

"One of the things I love most about Mima is her cooking."
Janelle Audrey Marrero – great-granddaughter

Mima says the Franco family had different traditions, like having *café con
leche* (Cuban coffee with milk) after dinner every night. "They were Catholic,
and they couldn't eat meat on Fridays, so every Friday they would ask me to
make a variety of dishes using codfish. Even though I'd never made some of the
dishes they requested, I learned quickly, and they loved everything I cooked."

*"Mima's cooking is incredible, even when it's something as simple as café
con leche. She taught me to genuinely care about others, and one way I do
that is through cooking, too."*
Adrian Fernandez (Boly) – grandson

When Francisca had to take a trip to Spain to see her family, she asked Mima
to take care of her husband, kids, and house. This was a sign of great trust.

When Francisca returned, she brought Mima several gifts from Spain,
including a box of Spanish sausages and other gourmet foods, which Mima
shared with her parents and siblings.

Gift of Leadership

In 1959, a local man said he wanted to create a farming cooperative to breed
hens in cages. Mima says she's not sure exactly how or why, but she was selected
to travel to Havana with him and a few other leaders from their community.

"We were even featured in a Cuban magazine called 'Bohemia,'" she says
with excitement. "That was my first time in Havana." She was 22 years old.

Mima said she would go, but only if she could take her mother with her, and
the director agreed. Her mother had a large goiter, and she had not been able to
see a doctor. Mima was hopeful that they could get her treatment in Havana.

The group slept at a *casa de huéspedes* (boarding house) and went around telling people about their farming cooperative, but Mima says no one wanted to hear about it.

"I don't know why, but we were wearing white jackets and hard hats. Wherever we went, people either ignored us or made fun of us. Eventually, the other participants got tired of it and went back home. But I wanted to stay to get help for my mother," she says.

One of the other participants was a very generous neighbor and family friend named Ricardo Hernández. Before leaving, he offered to speak to the owner of the boarding house so that Mima and her mother could stay there.

He even said he would cover their expenses, but Mima didn't want to take advantage of his kindness.

Mima took her mother to the hospital and spoke to the director.

"I knew he could tell she needed help, but he also knew we didn't have any money to pay for her treatment. I didn't know what he would do. He simply signed a form, and they admitted my mother," she says with amazement.

The surgery took a very long time, but it was successful. Afterwards, however, Mima says her mother was very weak.

At times, the doctors and nurses didn't think she would make it. She remained in the hospital for about two months due to various complications.

"I cried and prayed, prayed and cried... I didn't care if people saw me or heard me or called me crazy. I had faith that God would heal her," she says.

Mima says she quietly ate the leftovers from her mother's hospital meal tray each night. She was so hungry, but she couldn't afford to buy any food. And even more than that, she didn't want to leave her mother's bedside.

Every now and then, she would take the bus to her friend Manuela Franco's house for a quick shower and snack, and rush right back to the hospital.

Mima says a few weeks in, another patient's family was at the hospital during visiting hours, and a woman noticed that Mima was eating her mother's leftovers.

"She practically dragged me to the hospital cafeteria and bought me some food. Then she actually sat there and ate with me. I was overwhelmed with gratitude," she says.

When her mother was finally released from the hospital, Mima had no idea how she would pay for the trip back home, since the rest of their group had already left.

Manuela told her about a place where they provided help for people in need. Mima went to inquire, and she was able to get the two train passes for free.

"Because of that silly co-op, which never came to anything in the end, I was able to get my mother the surgery she'd needed for years! *Dios es grande.* (God is great.) You can overcome anything with faith," she says.

"My faith even filled my empty stomach on some of those nights."

"We finally arrived back home, and everyone was overjoyed to see my mother doing so well. My father even roasted a pig to celebrate that night. And my mother never had any other issues after that surgery," she adds, gratefully.

"Physically, I'm more like my dad, unfortunately for me! But I think I learned from Mima what it means to be a hard worker, take care of my family, love them and care for them. I wish I was half the woman she is. I love her so much and I'm very grateful for everything she has done for us."
María Teresa Suarez (Tere) – daughter

Chapter 3:
Confident Humility

Most of the families Mima worked for were good to her. But there were some exceptions. One woman she worked for, who was named Nancy, was married to a doctor and also studying to be a doctor herself.

Mima was hired to take care of their two daughters, and they required Mima to wear a uniform whenever they went out. Even one of their daughters, who was only 5 years old at the time, missed the bus one morning and refused to walk to school unless Mima put on her uniform first.

One night, when they were out at a social club for doctors, Nancy observed one of the doctors talking to Mima. After they left, she told Mima, "Don't even waste your time talking to him. He already has a girlfriend. And she's a nurse."

Mima says Nancy's mother would often bring "fancy" cheeses when she visited, and then blame Mima and the cook for eating them without permission.

Mima says she finally told Nancy she wouldn't eat those stinky, rotten cheeses – even if she hadn't eaten in 20 days!

"You can't let yourself be trampled on so easily," she reminds me, firmly.

One of the weekends that Mima was supposed to be off, just as she was heading out, Nancy asked her to stay. Mima tried to explain that she'd already made plans, but Nancy said, "If you leave now, you'll no longer work here."

She called the staffing agency to request a new nanny, right then and there.

It was that fateful moment that would lead Mima to meet her future husband.

After she was dismissed by Nancy, Mima went to stay with a friend named Marta in Marianao, in the province of Havana. Mima started working with a seamstress, who mentioned that one of her clients was looking for someone to clean her apartment, and she gave Mima the address.

Mima knocked on the door, and Basilia Domínguez (Cia, who would later become Mima's mother-in-law) answered the door. Cia let Mima in before she was done introducing herself.

Cia's daughter, Estela Roque (who was known as Estelita) was waiting for her hairdresser, and Cia let Mima in, thinking it was her. When Estelita came out, they were all very confused! Mima nervously explained why she was there, and Cia and Estelita told her to come back on Monday to see if it worked out.

So she did, and it did.

Once Cia got to know Mima, she would tell her youngest son, Eusebio Herrera – known to most of us as Pipo – about the endearing, beautiful, hard-working *guajirita* (country girl) who was working for Estelita.

"Pipo would hear her talking about me, and envision an ugly, toothless peasant. He'd always wanted to marry a *habanera* (city girl from Havana) with blonde hair and thick, beautiful legs," she says sarcastically.

A few weeks later, Cia announced that Eusebio was coming over for lunch.

"*Se volvió loco desde el primer día que me vio.* (He was crazy about me from the first day that he saw me.) I thought he was handsome, although he wasn't my type. But he had a lot of personality. He was serious and respectful. I was never into those immature guys and their *guanajería* (foolishness)," she says.

Left to right: Cruz María Herrera (Mima); Eusebio Herrera (Pipo), in the dark jacket, with some of his friends; Eusebio Herrera (Pipo) and Cruz María Herrera (Mima).

"He said he wanted to take me to the movies once. I said no, but he insisted and said 'I'll see you at the theater on Belascoaín Street.' Well, I didn't go, and as he stood outside waiting for me, it started to rain. He ran home, covering his head with a newspaper," she says. "But I'd told him I wasn't going!"

They eventually did go on dates... with Cia as their chaperone. Mima says Pipo loved taking her out to restaurants, carnivals, movies and comedy shows. He also liked to go dancing. She didn't, but he would still take her along.

"*Al que le gusta el baile, no hay quien lo pare.* (When someone loves dancing, there's no stopping them.) Later, I found out when he said he was going to the bathroom, he would leave me to find someone else to dance with," she says.

Pipo wanted to get married right away. Mima insisted that he didn't know anything about her, but he didn't care, and he was persistent. "He would tell me, 'I only care about your life from now on. I can't live another day without you.'"

Mima could see that he was pursuing her with good intentions.

"After a while, I did fall in love with him. We got married just nine months after we met. It would have been even sooner, if Cia hadn't convinced him to take some time to plan the wedding and fix up the apartment," she says.

So Mima ended up working for Estelita just a few months. With the wedding approaching, they didn't want other family or friends to see Mima as "the help," so Mima went to live with Pipo's oldest sister, Evelia Montes de Oca (known to most of us as Cuca) while they prepared for the wedding.

At the age of 24, Mima went to the beach for the first time with Cuca.

"I had lived on an island my whole life, and I didn't even know what the beach was like. Cuca let me borrow a bathing suit and some sunglasses. I didn't want to move from the shoreline, because I was scared I would drown," she says.

Close-Knit Family

"I wanted to go see my family before the wedding, to tell my parents in person, but I couldn't afford it. Pipo said we could go together after the wedding. I think he was afraid I would get cold feet if I went home," she says.

"So I wrote to let them know about the wedding, although I knew they couldn't come. I asked my cousin Paco, who was like my brother, to be there."

Left to right: Cruz María Herrera (Mima); Cruz María Herrera (Mima) and Paco Espinosa; Evelia Montes de Oca (Cuca), Eusebio Herrera (Pipo), Eusebio Herrera, Sr. (Can), Cruz María Herrera (Mima), Estela Roque (Estelita) and Basilia Domínguez (Cia); Eusebio Herrera (Pipo) and Cruz María Herrera (Mima).

Mima and Pipo got married on December 19, 1960 at Cuca's house.

Mima bought the fabric for her dress, and made it herself with some help from the seamstress she'd worked for. Estelita bought the cake, Cuca provided the drinks, and a notary named Victor married them.

Pipo's brother, Ernesto Herrera, hired the photographer.

"They said Ernesto was having a drink, and suddenly remembered the wedding. So he went to get the photographer, who we think was in the middle of another shoot, and they got there just in time," she says, laughing.

About four months after the wedding, Mima went to see her family and brought Pipo along to meet them. It was a long and anxious train ride for her.

"As we got closer, I'd tell him, 'That *bohío* (hut) looks like my house.' But he didn't believe me until we arrived and he saw it for himself."

Mima says her parents and siblings welcomed them excitedly, prepared special meals for them, and made Pipo feel comfortable. She remembers her mother turning the house upside down looking for a good fork for him to use!

"My family has always been very close, and very special to me. It was really important to me that Pipo could see that for himself," she says.

> *"I love being with the family, like Mima. It doesn't matter what we are doing. If we are together, we are having a good time."*
> *Jonathan Herrera (Jonny) – grandson*

After the wedding, Mima and Pipo lived in an apartment in Havana with Cia, who eventually moved out to live with two of her sisters.

Pipo worked as a *chapista* (auto body repairman) for the Revolutionary National Police. And they lived happily ever after...

Not quite.

That's where the story gets even more interesting.

Chapter 4:
Joys and Hardships

After launching a revolution that lasted several years, Fidel Castro had ousted Cuba's military dictator, Fulgencio Batista, just a few years before (on December 31, 1958).

Not long after Mima and Pipo got married, Cia, Ernesto, Cuca, Estelita, and their families came to the U.S., fleeing from Castro's regime. Mima says they tried to convince her and Pipo to leave, too, but Pipo didn't want to. Like many Cubans, he believed in Castro's assurance of a brighter future for Cuba.

Mima also had high hopes for raising a family of her own in a city like Havana, which was very different from her own upbringing.

"I prayed that God would help me, so that when I became a mother, my kids could have a better life. I didn't want them to go through what I went through."

A few months later, Mima returned to see her family again – and to face a devastating loss. Uvaldito, one of her youngest brothers, had died in an accident.

Mima initially heard that he was in critical condition. It was September 24, 1961 and she was getting close to the end of her first pregnancy. She was scared she'd go into labor so far away from home, but she decided to go anyway.

"When I arrived, and I saw so many people at the house, I knew. Something terrible had happened. My mother tried to console me. She was concerned for me because of the pregnancy. But even though I was not a mother yet, I could see her pain. She was never the same after that," she says, tearfully.

Just a few days later, on October 16, 1961, Mima experienced the wonder of becoming a mother. She was 25 years old.

She gave birth to her first child, María Teresa (my mother, known to most people as Tere), at the *Hospital Militar* (Military Hospital) in Havana.

"Because of my younger siblings, I had an idea of what to expect. But I quickly realized that having children of my own was going to be very different. The love you have for your children is a special kind of love. It is indescribable. It is unlike any other love," she says, with a bright smile.

"Tere heard everyone call me 'María,' and started to call me that, too," Mima says. "Although it sounded more like 'Iíííía.' Finally, our neighbor – Caristina, who was Tere's godmother – taught her to call me 'Mima.' And that was it!"

Cruz María Herrera (Mima), María Teresa Suarez (Tere) and Eusebio Herrera (Pipo).

Her next two babies, Clara Aurora (known to most of us as Toti), and María Caridad (known to most of us as Cary), were both in a breech position at birth, although Mima and her doctors didn't know it until she was in active labor.

When she was in labor with Toti at the *Clínica Asociación Cubana* (Cuban Association Clinic), Mima says the midwife came to check on her, and said with a puzzled expression, "Wait just a moment..."

She left and came back with one of the doctors, telling him, "*Mire eso. Eso no es cabeza.*" (Look at that. That's not a head.) She was coming out bottom first!

Toti was born on March 8, 1963, when Mima was 26 years old.

"Because I was born on International Women's Day, Pipo wanted to name me after Clara Zetkin, a Socialist leader from Germany who'd proposed the observance of that holiday. Mima wanted to name me after her mother, who we all knew as 'Aurora.' It wasn't until several years later, when Mima was visiting her family, that she happened to see her mother's I.D. and realized her full name was actually 'Clara Aurora,' too. I never really liked my name before that, but when Mima told me, I was so happy."
Clara Aurora Matos (Toti) – daughter

Left to right: Clara Aurora Matos (Toti) and María Teresa Suarez (Tere); Eusebio Herrera (Pipo), María Teresa Suarez (Tere), Clara Aurora Matos (Toti) and Cruz María Herrera (Mima).

When Mima was pregnant with Cary, her mother and younger brother, Rey, had come to visit her in Havana. When she went into labor, her mother stayed home with Tere and Toti, and Mima went to the *Hospital Nacional* (National Hospital) in Havana with Pipo and Rey.

It was her most difficult delivery. During the pregnancy, Mima says she had been nauseous and turned off by most foods, so she was very weak. Her anemia had gotten so bad that she'd even needed a blood transfusion.

"Even though Cary was tiny, since she was breech, every time she was close to coming out, she would push back up with her feet. They eventually had to bring in a nurse to sit above my belly and push her down."

Chuckling, she adds, "The doctor told me, '*¡Prepárate!* (Get ready!) The first thing she showed the world is her bottom. She's going to be a feisty one!'"

Cary was born on June 15, 1965, when Mima was 29 years old.

Even though Cary was born on time, she weighed just 4 pounds, so she had to stay in the hospital a little longer. Mima was very frail and needed another blood transfusion. She was also fighting a kidney infection and a persistent fever.

Mima says she had not been able to nurse Tere or Toti, but since Cary was very weak and underweight, the nurses insisted that she try.

When Mima put Cary to her breast, she says she almost immediately started to feel faint. *"Iba pa' el piso con niña y todo."* (I was headed to the floor with the baby and all.) Thankfully, one of the other ladies in the maternity ward noticed, and quickly ran to catch Cary before she hit the ground.

So she bottle-fed Cary with baby formula at first, and eventually evaporated milk diluted with water. Mima says she gained weight and grew quickly.

"She ate non-stop and cried whenever I stopped feeding her. Poor thing! I think she was so hungry because I hardly ate during my pregnancy."

Left to right: Clara Aurora Matos (Toti) and María Teresa Suarez (Tere); María Caridad García (Cary); Clara Aurora Matos (Toti) and María Caridad García (Cary).

Mima and Pipo eventually moved to a house in Santiago de las Vegas, *"en la Calle 6, entre 15 y 17"* (6th Street, between 15th and 17th Streets), part of the municipality of Boyeros.

Weary from the hardship and deprivation they faced day after day, Pipo became disillusioned with Castro's broken promises to bring freedom and stability to the Cuban people.

Just a few years before, he had been through a four-week military training. He had enthusiastically supported the Revolution and proudly reported to work in a military uniform each day. But he was beginning to see things differently. He resented the oppressive, Communist dictatorship they lived under.

This all came to a head in the summer of 1967.

A neighbor had informed the government that she suspected Pipo had a passport, and that Mima had an image of Cuba's patron saint, *La Virgen de la Caridad* (Our Lady of Charity) in the house.

These were considered serious violations, and even more so for someone in Pipo's position. He was summoned by one of the lieutenants and given a stern warning. Not long after that, when he spoke up against extended work hours at a meeting, he was told, "If it doesn't suit you, prepare to face the consequences."

Pipo recalls:

> *"About a month after that, I requested a discharge. But I knew they weren't going to release me. I found out that a few of my cousins were planning to leave Cuba, and decided that if I could make it to the U.S. and be reunited with my family, I could eventually petition to have Mima and the kids join me. Around mid-morning one day, my aunt Felicia called the shop and said, 'Your daughter, Clara, is sick. You need to go to the hospital.' That was the code! The others were waiting for me at a beach in the northern part of Pinar del Río. We were in hiding for four days before setting out early one morning. I knew they would come looking for me after just one day. They would have considered me a deserter. But I had already instructed Mima to say she didn't know anything."*

Pipo says their boat was only 2-3 miles off the coast when the engine began to fail. As they were trying to fix it, they could see a passenger ferry approaching, so they pulled out fishing rods and pretended they were fishing.

The ferry kept going, and they all breathed a sigh of relief.

But all of a sudden, it turned back. Just as they got the boat's motor to work again, they realized there was a platoon of police officers aboard the ferry. The officers began to fire. Thankfully, none of them were hit, but they surrendered and were taken into custody.

Mima says she hadn't heard from Pipo in more than five days when they notified her that he'd been imprisoned.

"They gave me a specific date to go see him, and I went with all three girls," she says. They were only 6, 4, and 2 years old.

Mima was about three months pregnant with her fourth child. She and Pipo both knew it already, but no one else knew, since she wasn't showing yet.

"People can be so malicious. Once my belly began to grow, the rumors started swirling."

"Remember this," she adds, leaning in. "Many people are willing to speak negatively about others. But saying something kind, or recognizing someone's good character... well, that doesn't come so easily. That's why you have to be sure of who you are and not let those things get to you."

Mima says some people even brazenly told her she shouldn't have the baby. But she wouldn't listen to them.

"It wasn't the baby's fault that I already had three kids, or that my husband was in prison. We have to trust God in the face of fear. Never do something out of fear that you might later regret."

Mima says that when she went into labor, a neighbor and very good friend named Felicia Placeres (who was known as Fela) called a taxi for her. Fela rode with Mima to the hospital, but couldn't stay because she had a very bad cold, so she took the taxi back home.

A few months after Pipo went to prison, Mima gave birth to her fourth child all alone. She was 31 years old when Waldo Ramón (known to most of us as Papito), was born on February 1, 1968 at the hospital in Boyeros.

Afterwards, she says, she couldn't believe how many people went to visit her in the hospital. Even the neighborhood grocer stopped by! A friend ultimately explained that they all wanted to see if Papito looked like Pipo or not.

"And they couldn't say anything other than, 'Wow, he looks just like your husband.'" she recalls. "He really is like a mirror image of Pipo."

She smiles, and says about Papito, *"Mira a mi niño, tan bello que está, y cómo me quiere."* (Look at my boy, how handsome he is, and how much he loves me.)

> *"I go by every day after work and make coffee for her. She always waits for me with a big smile. I love sitting, talking and laughing with her while we sip the coffee in our special mugs. I told her those two mugs are only for her and me, and when we're done, I wash them and put them away safely so no one else will use them."*
> *Waldo Ramón Herrera (Papito) – son*

Left to right: Waldo Ramón Herrera (Papito) and Cruz María Herrera (Mima); Clara Aurora Matos (Toti), Waldo Ramón Herrera (Papito), Cruz María Herrera (Mima), María Caridad García (Cary) and María Teresa Suarez (Tere).

The next day, the hospital released her and called a taxi to take her and the new baby home. "When I walked out, all alone with the baby," she says, a knot forming in her throat (and mine), "I was overcome with so many emotions."

"Tears welled up in my eyes, but by the time the taxi drove up to our house, I had pulled myself together. The three girls were with my sister, who had come to take care of them, and they were so excited to welcome their brother home."

"The next day, I went right back to cleaning, washing, cooking, and all the rest, as if I had not just given birth. God has always given me good health and the strength to keep going," she says.

Shortly after he was born, she took Papito to the prison so Pipo could meet his son. Later, when Pipo was transferred to a prison that was closer to their house, she would go with all four kids, or sometimes with just Cary and Papito.

"I wanted them to know who their father was and to see him regularly. It wasn't easy. They were so little. By the time we got there, sometimes they'd thrown up, or spilled their water on me. But it was worth it. When a child is raised with the love of a mother and a father, it makes a difference."

Pipo was sentenced to 12 years, and ultimately served 8 years, as a *preso político* (political prisoner) for his act of "treason."

He was transferred to several different prisons during that time – La Cabaña, Villa Marista, El Castillo del Príncipe, Puerto Boniato, and Melena. He also worked in the sugar cane fields in the town of Manatí for about 11 months, and did auto body repairs in the town of Jaruco for four years as part of his sentence.

Mima remained faithful and steadfast, trusting God, honoring her commitment to him, and doing whatever was necessary to care for and provide for her children.

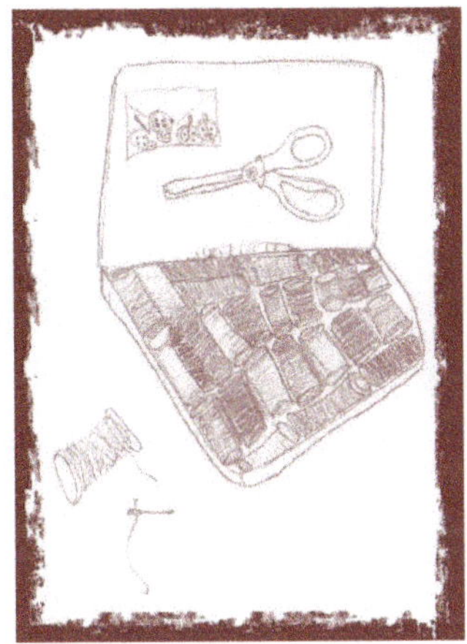

"When the kids were little, I worked non-stop. I would help seamstresses with sewing jobs. I would wash and iron clothes for people. I would make *croquetas* (croquettes) and fruit juices to sell to the neighbors," she says.

"We always ate dinner early. Then I would give the kids a bath, and get them ready for bed," she says. "They all wanted to sleep with me, so I would put the three girls on my bed, pull Papito's crib close to the edge, and just stretch out my arm so he could grab my hand. I'd lay there until they all fell asleep."

"After they were asleep, I'd quietly get out of the bed and get to work. I did all of this at night while they slept, so I didn't get much sleep," she adds.

"Sometimes, while I was out hanging clothes to dry, I could hear my neighbors leaving to go to work for the day, and I'd still been up without sleeping from the night before," she says. "I think that's why I love to sleep so much now! *Sueño viejo...* (Making up for lost sleep...) Now, I take a nap every day."

"One thing I have in common with Mima is that we both like to sleep."
Daniel Matos (Danny) – grandson

Despite the Cuban government's rationing system – in which the *libreta* (ration booklet) dictated what they could buy – Mima says she improvised and did what she could with what they had. She still prepared delicious meals for her kids, stretched ingredients to make and sell her coveted homemade treats, and made it a point to celebrate memorable moments.

"Whenever we made plans to go to the beach, I would stay up late the night before making *pollo asado* (oven-roasted chicken), rice, beans and *platanitos* (fried sweet plantains)," she says.

"I'd pack everything, wake up the kids, get them ready, and take them on the one-hour trek. We usually rode on a *camión* (dump truck) that was used for transportation, along with dozens of other people going to the beach."

"By the time we got there, the kids couldn't wait to eat. They had been smelling the food the whole ride – along with everyone else on the truck!"

"And then of course, they had to wait an hour after eating before getting in the water. By the time they actually started swimming and playing, it was time to go back home," she says, shaking her head and laughing.

Mima says she would take the kids to Holguín as often as she could, both to visit her family, and also to expose them to the difficult realities of life in the countryside. In the midst of long, humid summers, her parents' old house – with its palm roof and dirt floor – would become a fun-filled adventure for some of them, and a slightly traumatizing experience for others.

"Papito would hop on a horse the moment we arrived. He loved every minute we spent there. Poor Tere would get attacked by mosquitoes and refuse to walk on the muddy floor. She got sick almost every time we went," she says.

For her kids' birthdays, Mima would always find a special way to celebrate. Papito even had a costume party one year!

She would make or buy a new outfit, hire a photographer, cook some special treats, and spend hours waiting in line at the *bodega* (neighborhood market).

Left to right: Waldo Ramón Herrera (Papito); Clara Aurora Matos (Toti), María Caridad García (Cary), Waldo Ramón Herrera (Papito) and María Teresa Suarez (Tere).

"For birthdays, we could buy a cake and soda. But I had to go early to make sure I got it before they ran out," she says.

"With the *libreta* (ration booklet), we had limited access to basics like soap, rice, eggs, sugar and milk. Even shoes and underwear were rationed. Sure, it was hard, but we are not put on this earth to give up when things are hard," she adds.

Enduring Faith

During that time, students in 7th to 12th grades were also required to do "voluntary" agricultural work for 45 days each year. Yes, you read that right – required and voluntary.

Tere and Toti participated in the *Escuela al Campo* (School in the Countryside) program a few times, and Cary also went one year.

Mima would travel to see them on Sundays, always arriving with a warm embrace and homemade treats to hold them over until her next visit.

Toti recalls:

> *"Mima went through a lot, gathering food and supplies to help sustain us, and then traveling for hours in difficult conditions to get to us. Believe it or not, I actually have some good memories from that time. Aside from the fact that we had to work really hard, we did have fun with our friends. We were young and easily adapted to our surroundings. But the visits from Mima were definitely the highlight at the end of each week."*

Mima says she is thankful for the many good friends she and the kids had in their neighborhood. Mima's family lived several hours away, and Pipo's family was already in the U.S., but these friends were truly like family.

Aside from her friend Fela (and her husband Roberto), Ana Delgado and Leticia Delgado were also there to lend a helping hand, take care of the kids, or just offer moral support as she juggled so many responsibilities on her own.

Left to right: María Teresa Suarez (Tere) and Clara Aurora Matos (Toti); Clara Aurora Matos (Toti), Eusebio Herrera (Pipo) and María Teresa Suarez (Tere); María Teresa Suarez (Tere), María Caridad García (Cary) and Clara Aurora Matos (Toti).

Even though she didn't grow up going to church, Mima says she always believed in God, asked him for help, and trusted that he had a plan.

"The things I have seen God do have been amazing," she says.

Fela was the one who first introduced Mima to Christianity and took the kids to the Methodist church with her (Iglesia Metodista de Santiago de las Vegas).

Mima says Tere, Toti and Cary had all been baptized in the Catholic Church as babies. Papito was later baptized at the age of 12. But neither Mima or Pipo went to church regularly or considered themselves devout Catholics.

"Many people were surprised that we'd baptized them. Since Pipo was with the government, they assumed we didn't believe in God. Religion went against the government's atheist philosophy."

Going to the Methodist church with Fela was an important part of her faith formation (and that of her kids) while Pipo was in prison.

Mima says religious persecution was common during that time. "We weren't fearful, but many people felt that being known as a Christian would be detrimental to their reputations or access to education and opportunities."

"Despite all that, I'm thankful for Fela's faith and influence, and to now have the assurance that all my children love God and believe in him," she says.

Mima says her four kids loved each other and got along well, for the most part. "Cary took care of Papito as if he were her baby, even though she wasn't much older! Tere and Toti were very close in age, but they clashed a lot more."

"I would tell them over and over, 'God made siblings to love and care for one another.' They struggled through that concept for a few years, but now look at them. Inseparable! All four of them are inseparable," she says.

"And I've been blessed, because all of my children – whenever I've had something important to teach them – listened to me. They still do. I've always tried not to fuss at them, but ultimately help them understand what is right."

Left to right: Clara Aurora Matos (Toti), Cruz María Herrera (Mima), María Caridad García (Cary), Eusebio Herrera (Pipo), Waldo Ramón Herrera (Papito) and María Teresa Suarez (Tere); María Teresa Suarez (Tere) and Clara Aurora Matos (Toti).

Chapter 5:
Courageous Spirit

When they finally had the opportunity to leave Cuba in 1980 – 13 long and hard years after Pipo was arrested and imprisoned – Mima says they knew it was the right decision. But leaving everything behind, including Mima's family, and friends who were like family, was a very emotional process.

They desperately wanted to leave before Papito turned 16, since he would be required to enlist in the Cuban military. As a former political prisoner, Pipo had been granted asylum, which also covered Mima, Cary and Papito. But they needed to come up with another plan for Tere and Toti, who were already older.

They'd heard that a crowd was gathering at the Peruvian Embassy to request asylum. After talking it through with Pipo, Tere and Toti arrived at the embassy, not knowing how long they'd be there, or what the outcome would be.

Over the next few days, the crowd grew to more than 10,000 people. Sandwiched between strangers, united by hope, the two of them sat back-to-back on the embassy's lawn for hours on end. They didn't have any food other than some sugar water that a kind older lady shared to keep them from fainting.

After two weeks, they left the embassy, passports in hand, hearts full of anticipation, and a box lunch they couldn't even eat – their jaws hurt too much after not chewing for so long. The government eventually announced that the Port of Mariel would be opened for anyone who wanted to leave the country.

Tere recalls:

"My life, and that of my descendants, changed forever on that day. I'm beyond grateful that none of our younger generation had to live through what we did. Outside the gates of the embassy, the mob was chanting, '¡Que se vayan! (Let them leave!) Get out, traitors! Out with the scum!' and throwing things at us. Finally, those boats you've seen in the news reports brought the first six Herreras to Miami. What a journey! We made history – and I would do it all over again. This is why we don't take freedom for granted and we are so thankful to God and to this country."

Mima had gone to visit her family in Holguín a few weeks before, and the family encouraged her mother to go spend some time with Mima in Havana.

"My mother arrived, and within three days, we got word that we had gotten final approval to leave. I kissed my mother, and hugged her tightly. I could feel her trembling, and I said *'No te preocupes.* (Don't worry.) Maybe they just need us to fill out some papers. We might be back...'"

Mima says leaving her mother and niece, Nury Cruz, behind that day was one of the most difficult moments of her life.

"I had been taking care of Nury, as one of my own daughters. Her mother was my sister, Aurorita, who had died. I wanted to bring Nury with me, but she wasn't my biological child."

"So we left the two of them at our house and went on our way."

"And I never got to see my mother again," she says. "That's the one thing I still wish I could do today – hug my mother one more time."

It is hard to imagine what they all went through, especially Tere and Toti, who each came on different days, on separate boats, surrounded by strangers. Pipo, Mima, Cary and Papito all traveled together a few days later.

Left to right: Nury Cruz; Cruz María Herrera (Mima), María Teresa Suarez (Tere), Clara Aurora Matos (Toti), Waldo Ramón Herrera (Papito), María Caridad García (Cary) and Eusebio Herrera (Pipo).

Surviving the precarious 90-mile journey from Cuba to Key West, they eventually ended up at the Orange Bowl, where Miami officials had set up a temporary station to process the refugees and connect them to their relatives.

They were all reunited in Miami within days, which was not very common. It is estimated that more than 100,000 Cubans came to the U.S. through the Mariel Boatlift over a period of approximately five months.

Many families were separated for days or weeks in the midst of the chaos. Toti recalls:

"I arrived first, and immediately started volunteering at the Orange Bowl with one of my cousins. Each night, I would leave with pockets full of phone numbers and messages to relay to people's relatives. After about a week, I was making coffee one day, and they called me over the loudspeaker. Tere had arrived! About a week after that, I was helping at the fingerprinting station when the others arrived."

"Vinimos cuando Dios quiso que viniéramos. (We came when God wanted us to come.) Not a day before or a day after. It was his plan," Mima says confidently.

Tere was 18 years old, Toti was 17, Cary was almost 15, and Papito was 12.

Mima says she'd imagined the U.S. as something out of another world. "When I saw the people dressed 'normally' just like us, and walking 'normally' on two feet just like us... I was so relieved. Even the weather was the same!"

Many things were different, to be sure. "It was hard to think I might never see my family again. None of them ever made it to the U.S. And we arrived without a single thing, other than the clothes we were wearing," she says.

"I was 44 years old and starting from zero once again."

More than anything, they felt fortunate to be together and grateful for the love and support they received from Pipo's family.

They lived with Pipo's sister, Estelita, and her family, in Hialeah for a short time. Eventually, Tere and Toti stayed there, and the others moved in with Pipo's brother, Ernesto, and his family, who lived about 30 minutes away.

Evelia Montes de Oca (Cuca), Ernesto Herrera, Basilia Domínguez (Cia), Eusebio Herrera (Pipo) and Estela Roque (Estelita).

Left to right: Eusebio Herrera (Pipo) and Cruz María Herrera (Mima); Cruz María Herrera (Mima); María Caridad García (Cary) and Eusebio Herrera (Pipo); Cruz María Herrera (Mima) and Waldo Ramón Herrera (Papito); María Teresa Suarez (Tere) and Waldo Ramón Herrera (Papito); Clara Aurora Matos (Toti), Eusebio Herrera (Pipo) and María Caridad García (Cary).

Mima says that, while she was grateful for the family's help, she was anxious for them to have their own place. She would go out to look for houses with her sister-in-law, Walkyria Herrera. On one of those outings, they found a house they liked, and the rent was only $400 a month. And it even had a pool!

"Papito had been asking us to look for a house with a pool, and I never thought it would be possible," she says. The "pool house," as they still refer to it, became the Herrera family's very first home in the U.S.

Mima was not able to return to Cuba for 13 years, because the Cuban government forbade visits from the "deserters" who'd left. Mima's mother died just seven months prior to her first trip back in 1993, once the restrictions were lifted. Still, Mima rejoiced at the opportunity to see her family again.

"It was like a dream. I was so happy to see my father, siblings and other family. Many who were little when we left had families of their own! We stayed up late, laughing and telling old stories. We love to laugh," she says.

"I definitely got my sense of humor from Mima's side of the family. They are always laughing. You'll never know if it's going to be at you, or with you, and you can't help but laugh either way."
Waldo Ramón Herrera (Papito) – son

Left to right: Emelina Espinosa, Aida Espinosa and Rey Espinosa; Cruz María Herrera (Mima), Emelina Espinosa, Juan Espinosa, Elda Espinosa and Aida Espinosa; Atilano Espinosa (Nan), Aida Espinosa, Renán Espinosa, Juan Espinosa, Emelina Espinosa, Elda Espinosa and Cruz María Herrera (Mima).

"For 10 years, I was able to go see my father, spend time with him, and help provide the medications he needed before he passed away," she says.

As a former political prisoner, Pipo, on the other hand, has never returned to Cuba. As a kid, I always remember hearing him say he would only go *cuando se caiga Fidel* (after the fall of Fidel), and wondering... *What exactly is Fidel on top of? Did he climb up a big tree? And why are we all waiting for him to fall?*

It just so happened that when Castro died on November 25, 2016, Mima and Pipo were at my home in North Carolina. They had come with my parents and some other family members to spend the Thanksgiving holiday with us.

I remember my mother coming to the kitchen table where Pipo was having breakfast, and telling him, *"Hay noticias de Cuba... Se murió Fidel."* (There's some news from Cuba... Fidel died.) His shocked and tearful reaction – a mix of anger for the years taken from him, longing for something better, and relief for those who'd suffered like him – is something I will never forget.

Prudent Stewardship

After some time at the "pool house," Mima and Pipo moved in with Tere and her husband in Princeton; later on, they rented another house in Perrine; and finally, they moved in with Toti and her husband in South Miami Heights.

"When we lived with Toti and Pele, I started taking care of kids," Mima says. "Some days, I would have up to 10 kids at a time!"

Mima continued to take care of many children through the years, from her own grandchildren to the children of neighbors and friends from church. Over the years, she cared for more than 30 children, until she retired in 2002.

"Mima is always loving and caring towards others. I remember how she used to take care of us when we were little. She always made us take naps, and sometimes we'd pretend to give her a massage just to stay up longer."
Kevin Herrera – grandson

"Some of the kids were with me all day, from breakfast through lunch and nap time, to dinner and bath time at night. Sometimes, I'd even send the parents home with dinner. I knew they'd be tired after a long day at work," she says.

"I have always loved kids and wanted to have a big family. Some of the kids I took care of, and their parents, have become like part of our family," she adds.

Many of them still call to check on her, or stop by to bring her flowers for her birthday. Her front door is always open, and her kitchen is always stocked with the essentials to quickly whip up some comfort food for whoever stops by.

"I will always appreciate Mima's hospitality and smile. She is caring towards others, no matter what."
Alain Fernandez – grandson

Mima and Pipo didn't have high-profile jobs or big salaries. But they worked hard, paid their bills, saved money and always helped those in need. Between Pipo's job as an auto body repairman, and the money she made from babysitting, they were able to buy their own house in 1987.

"I had to learn early on how to manage money, not only for myself, but also to help my family. That has helped me my whole life. A sheet of paper and a pencil is all you need to balance it all out," she says.

"Something I learned from Mima is the importance of saving and managing money well."
Daniel Matos (Danny) – grandson

In 2016, they paid off their house, something many Americans only ever dream of accomplishing. And speaking of the "American Dream," Mima and Pipo became naturalized U.S. citizens in 2008.

"This country has provided the freedom and opportunities for our family that we could only dream of in Cuba," she says.

Chapter 6:
Nurturing Heart

Mima became a grandmother at the age of 45, when I was born on October 12, 1981. "It was like having kids all over again. I love being a grandmother," she says.

"What I love most is that I have been able to see my 10 grandchildren grow and help take care of all of them."

On April 29, 2009, she became a great-grandmother when my daughters, Janelle and Julianna, were born. Mima says she'd always wanted to have twins, and when she didn't, she hoped someday one of her daughters might.

They didn't, either, but at the age of 72, she finally got her twins.

"*¡Qué emoción!* (How exciting!) I always say those are *my* twins, because I prayed for them for so many years," she says.

The family keeps growing, and she is loving every minute of it. When I ask her what she's most proud of, she wisely responds with a different phrase.

"The thing I am most *thankful* to God for, and that fills me with the most joy is my family. My children, my grandchildren, my great-grandchildren... I had a difficult childhood, but I'm thankful that I've been blessed to live into my 80s, and I've seen many beautiful things in my life."

Indeed, over the years, she has been to countless little league baseball games, ballet recitals, church pageants, birthday parties, baptisms, weddings, baby showers, school plays and graduations.

She has also witnessed and comforted us in our suffering – from broken hearts to emergency room visits.

In short, Mima has been a part of just about every important milestone in our lives.

"I know having a family like this is rare. We love each other deeply, without fighting over things that are not important. We love to be together," she says.

"*¡Oye! Cuatro generaciones... Eso no es fácil.* (Listen! Four generations... That's not easy.) People have often asked me, 'How did you do it?' I give thanks to God."

It also warms her heart to see the legacy her children are already carrying on.

Tere makes it a point to celebrate memorable moments with the family, from holidays and birthdays to all-out family reunions.

Toti and Pele's house – which we all refer to as *La Finca* (The Farm) – is always ready to welcome guests and has become the official gathering spot for special celebrations, for family and friends alike.

Toti's *congrí* (rice and black beans) has already been said to taste... just like Mima's!

Cary and Papito are also known for their delicious cooking and *cafecito* (coffee).

And at the rate Papito and Maggie's family is growing, their grandchildren will soon outnumber Mima and Pipo's!

I know through the years, the rest of us will also carry on what we've learned from Mima through *our* families, homes and traditions.

Words of Wisdom

It's our last night in Naples. Mima and I are both noticeably tired and energized at the same time. Early tomorrow morning, my family and I will drive back home to North Carolina. I am feeling grateful for the time we've enjoyed together, and as always, already dreading the emotional good-byes.

My husband and girls come into the room to check on us and kiss us goodnight, but she keeps talking, and I can't stop listening.

Mima never learned to speak English. She never learned to drive. She never learned algebra, or chemistry, or how to use a computer. But she is one of the most insightful and discerning people many of us have ever known.

"I give thanks to God for giving me the wisdom and good sense to make the right decisions, and to advise my siblings, kids and grandkids along the right path," she says.

> *"One of the things I admire about Mima is her wisdom. I love it when my mom tells us stories about Mima. It always makes me smile."*
> *Julianna Beatriz Marrero – great-granddaughter*

As we are wrapping up, I ask her if she wants to share any words of advice with those who will someday read this, and she responds, without hesitation, "First of all, have faith in God."

"And if you get married and start a family of your own, choose your spouse by their character, not by their beauty. That fades away."

"Work together and do the best that you can for your family to have a good, healthy, stable upbringing. You have to fight for the things that are important to you."

"*Lo que tú no puedas arreglar, ponlo en las manos de Dios. Él sí puede.* (When there is a situation you cannot fix, put it in God's hands. He can.) I know that's a really long answer, but that's what I think," she concludes.

Mima's childhood dream was to become either a nurse or a teacher. She has always had a heart for people.

"My family could never afford to go to the doctor, so I was their 'nurse.' And I've been a 'teacher' for all my siblings, kids, grandkids, and even many friends."

She smiles, *"No me puedo quejar."* (I can't complain.)

As one of her "students," I can say with certainty that while she may not have always *intended* to teach us a lesson, the way she lives always teaches us *something*.

Left to right: Eusebio Herrera (Pipo) and Cruz María Herrera (Mima);
María Teresa Suarez (Tere), Cruz María Herrera (Mima), María Caridad García (Cary), Waldo Ramón
Herrera (Papito), Clara Aurora Matos (Toti) and Eusebio Herrera (Pipo);
Cruz María Herrera (Mima) and Eusebio Herrera (Pipo);
María Caridad García (Cary), Clara Aurora Matos (Toti), Cruz María Herrera (Mima), Eusebio Herrera
(Pipo), María Teresa Suarez (Tere) and Waldo Ramón Herrera (Papito);
Children and Spouses – Waldo Ramón (Papito) and Magali Zayas Herrera ("Big" Maggie), Rolando
(Roly) and María Teresa Suarez (Tere), Eusebio (Pipo) and Cruz María Herrera (Mima), Clara Aurora
(Toti) and Pelayo Matos (Pele), María Caridad (Cary) and Jorge García.

Left to right: Grandchildren – Adrian Fernandez (Boly), Karina Gudiel, Emmanuel Matos (Manny), Cruz María Herrera (Mima), Daniel Matos (Danny), Eusebio Herrera (Pipo), Alain Fernandez, Natalie Caridad Fernandez (Naty), Marilyn Marrero, Maggie Cruz ("Baby" Maggie), Kevin Herrera and Jonathan Herrera (Jonny);
Great-Grandchildren – Julianna Beatriz Marrero, Cruz María Herrera (Mima), Kevin Alexander Herrera ("Baby" Kevin), Eusebio Herrera (Pipo), Anna Carolina Gudiel (Annie), Janelle Audrey Marrero and Emma Grace Gudiel; Anna Carolina Gudiel (Annie), Emma Grace Gudiel, Camila Rose Herrera, Leah Rae Herrera, Aubrey Lynn Herrera and Kevin Alexander Herrera ("Baby" Kevin);
"El Familión" Reunion – 2017; "El Familión" Reunion – 2018.

Cruz María Herrera (Mima), now (80s) and then (20s).

"Strength and dignity are her clothing;
And she laugheth at the time to come.
She openeth her mouth with wisdom;
And the law of kindness is on her tongue.
She looketh well to the ways of her household,
And eateth not the bread of idleness.
Her children rise up, and call her blessed;
Her husband also, and he praiseth her, saying:
Many daughters have done worthily,
But thou excellest them all.
Grace is deceitful, and beauty is vain;
But a woman that feareth Jehovah, she shall be praised.
Give her of the fruit of her hands;
And let her works praise her in the gates."
Proverbs 31: 25-31, ASV

PART TWO – MIMA'S RECIPES:
¡Buen Provecho! (Enjoy!)

Photo courtesy of Karina Gudiel.

Familión Favorites (Pages 52 - 63)
These are the dishes we each call our favorites from Mima's kitchen. It's so hard to choose just one or two. These are the ones Mima makes when it's your birthday, you're not feeling well, or you haven't been to her house in a while and she wants to make you something special. Next time you want someone to feel loved, invite them over and ask, just like Mima, "¿Qué quieres que te haga?" (What do you want me to make for you?)

Still Hungry? (Pages 64 - 76)
Let's be honest. If it's Mima's cooking, you just want to keep eating. Just like Mima says, "¿Te quedaste con hambre?" (Still hungry?) Have some more! These are other dishes we've enjoyed over the years at her house. Who knows? Someday they may be our kids' or grandkids' favorites.

Café con Leche (Cuban Coffee with Milk)

Serves 2 | 152 calories per serving | Favorite of: Jonathan Herrera (Jonny), Adrian Fernandez (Boly), Janelle Audrey Marrero and Julianna Beatriz Marrero

Ingredients:

1/2 cup of strong, brewed espresso

1-1/2 cups of whole milk

1 teaspoon of granulated sugar, or more, to taste

1. Brew the espresso according to the manufacturer's instructions.
2. Optional step: If you want to make it even better, right when the coffee starts brewing, pour the first few drops (about 1-2 teaspoons) into a mug with 2 tablespoons of sugar. Stir quickly until it makes the caramel-colored froth known as *espumita*. Add the rest of the brewed coffee and stir well.
3. Heat the milk on the stove or in the microwave, but do not let it boil.
4. Add the espresso and sugar and stir well.
5. Adjust the amount of sugar to each person's preference. You will need more or less sugar depending on how sweet you like your coffee, and whether you made the *espumita* or not, since it contains sugar.

Café con Leche (Cuban Coffee with Milk) | Torrejas con Almíbar (French Toast with Homemade Syrup) | "Pina y Yeli" (PB&J)

Torrejas con Almíbar (French Toast with Homemade Syrup)

Serves 4 | 306 calories per serving | Favorite of: Marilyn Marrero

Ingredients (Syrup):

1/2 cup of granulated sugar

1/2 cup of water

2 cinnamon sticks

Ingredients (French Toast):

3 large eggs

1/4 cup of 2% milk

2 tablespoons of butter (divided)

8 slices of thin white sandwich bread

Ground cinnamon, to taste

1. Add the water, sugar and cinnamon sticks to a small pot over medium-high heat and stir well.
2. Bring to a boil, while gently whisking, until the sugar dissolves completely. Discard the cinnamon sticks.
3. Reduce to medium-low heat and let it simmer for about 15 minutes, while whisking occasionally, until it thickens a bit. Keep in mind that it will continue to thicken while cooling.
4. Meanwhile, beat the eggs and milk in a large, shallow bowl.
5. Add 1 tablespoon of the butter to a large frying pan over medium heat.
6. Once the butter is melted and sizzling, begin to soak the bread slices in the egg mixture.
7. Add the coated bread slices to the pan and sprinkle with ground cinnamon. Cook for about 3 minutes on each side, until they are golden brown.
8. Repeat with the remaining bread slices, adding 1/2 tablespoon of butter to the pan between the batches as needed.
9. Pour the syrup over the *Torrejas* just before serving.

"Pina y Yeli" (PB&J) *

Serves 1 | 377 calories per serving | Favorite of: Emmanuel Matos (Manny) and Daniel Matos (Danny)

Ingredients:

2 slices of thin white sandwich bread

2 tablespoons of creamy peanut butter

1 tablespoon of jelly of choice

1. Toast the bread.
2. Take one slice of bread and spread the peanut butter evenly on it.
3. Take the other slice of the bread and do the same with the jelly.
4. Combine the 2 slices of bread and cut into 4 squares before serving.

* This is how we all remember hearing Mima say "peanut butter and jelly" when we were kids, and it's what both Manny and Danny still called it when asked to name their favorite dishes from her kitchen!

Arroz Blanco (White Rice)

Serves 8 | 183 calories per serving | Favorite of: Natalie Caridad Fernandez (Naty)

Ingredients:

2-3 cups of water *

2 teaspoons of salt

2 cups of long-grain white rice

1 tablespoon of oil of choice

(Recipe continued on next page.)

1. Wash the rice and drain it well.
2. * If using an electric rice cooker: Add in the water (use 2 cups), salt, rice and oil. Stir, cover and switch to "cook."
   If cooking in a pot on the stove: Add the water (use 3 cups) and salt first and bring to a boil over medium-high heat. Stir in the rice and oil and wait until it begins to simmer. Cover and set to low heat. Cook over low heat for 20 minutes, without opening the lid. Remove from heat.
3. Let the rice rest for about 10 minutes and gently fluff before serving.

Huevos Fritos (Fried Eggs)

Serves 2 | 218 calories per serving | Favorite of: Emmanuel Matos (Manny)

Ingredients:
1/4 cup of oil, for frying
4 large eggs
Salt, to taste

1. Add the oil to a small frying pan over medium heat.
2. Once the oil is hot, crack the egg and drop it carefully into the pan. You can cook 2 eggs at a time if you have enough space in the pan.
3. Cook the eggs until the edges start to get slightly bubbly and crispy, but do not flip them. Watch out for the oil splattering.
4. With a spatula or spoon, carefully splash some of the hot oil over the top of the eggs until you start to see a slight white coating form over the yolks. * Sprinkle with salt just before serving.

* Do not overcook the eggs, or the yolks will get too hard, and you will miss out on the best part: dipping some *pan cubano* (Cuban bread) in the yolk.

Arroz con Huevos Fritos (White Rice with Fried Eggs)

¡Prueba Esto! (Try This!) These eggs are not just for breakfast. Serve the fried eggs over *arroz blanco* (white rice) for **Arroz con Huevos Fritos (White Rice with Fried Eggs),** a quick and easy lunch or dinner.

Fufú de Plátano (Mashed Plantains)

Serves 2 | 326 calories per serving | Favorite of: Mima and Waldo Ramón Herrera (Papito)

Ingredients:
2 plantains (1 ripe, 1 green)
6 cups of water
Salt, to taste
2 tablespoons of butter

1. Choose a combination of plantains that are ripe and sweet (yellow with black spots) and others that are green for a sweet-savory combination.
2. Wash and carefully chop the unpeeled plantains into large 3-inch rounds.
3. Add the water to a medium-sized pot over high heat, along with the plantains and a dash of salt.
4. Bring to a boil, and then lower to medium-high heat. Let them cook for about 20 minutes, until they are soft. You will see the skin starting to separate from the ripe plantains.
5. Pull the plantains out into a large bowl or platter, reserving the hot water in the pot. Let the plantains cool slightly before carefully discarding the skin.
6. Start mashing the plantains, while gradually incorporating the butter, about 1 teaspoon at a time. If the consistency is too dry, you can add some of the reserved water you boiled them in. Sprinkle with salt before serving.

Fufú con Huevos Fritos (Mashed Plantains with Fried Eggs)

Add two fried eggs for **Fufú con Huevos Fritos (Mashed Plantains with Fried Eggs)**. It's a satisfying meal you can enjoy any time of day – and it's one of Mima's favorites!

Arroz Blanco (White Rice) | Fufú con Huevos Fritos (Mashed Plantains with Fried Eggs) | Platanitos (Fried Sweet Plantains)

Platanitos (Fried Sweet Plantains)

Serves 4 | 260 calories per serving | Favorite of: María Caridad García (Cary), Waldo Ramón Herrera (Papito), Jonathan Herrera (Jonny), Alain Fernandez and Natalie Caridad Fernandez (Naty)

Ingredients:
2 extra ripe plantains (yellow with plenty of black spots)
Oil, for frying

1. Peel and slice the plantains at a slight angle into thin, 1/2-inch rounds.
2. Cover about 1/3 of a frying pan with oil, enough for the plantains to be fully covered while frying, and set to medium-high heat.
3. Once the oil is hot, carefully add the sliced plantains in a single layer.
4. When the edges start to turn brown, flip them and cook them until they are evenly browned and caramelized all around.
5. Place the plantains on a paper towel to help absorb some of the excess oil while you finish cooking the rest.

Tortilla de Plátanos (Sweet Plantain Omelet)

Serves 4 | 225 calories per serving | Favorite of: Pipo

Ingredients:

1 extra ripe plantain (yellow with plenty of black spots), fried and lightly mashed

4 large eggs

2 tablespoons of 2% milk

1/4 teaspoon of salt

1 tablespoon of oil of choice

1. Beat the eggs, milk and salt in a bowl. Add the plantains and mix well.
2. Grease a small frying pan with the oil and set to medium-low heat.
3. Pour the egg mixture into the pan and spread out the plantains evenly.
4. Cook slowly over medium-low heat, so the bottom doesn't burn. Using a spatula, gently separate the edges of the omelet from the pan, tilt the pan slightly, and let the runny eggs flow towards the edges and under.
5. Once the center of the omelet is no longer runny, carefully flip the omelet onto a plate, so the cooked side is facing up, and then slide the uncooked side back into the pan.
6. Switch the heat to low and cook for about 5 more minutes, depending on the size of your pan and the thickness of your omelet, until it cooks completely.

Tortilla de Papas (Potato Omelet)

¡Prueba Esto! (Try This!) *Serves 3 | 237 calories per serving.* Fry 1 cup of diced potatoes in a small frying pan over medium-high heat, with 1/2 cup of oil, for about 8-10 minutes until they are golden and crispy. Replace the plantains in Step 1 with the potatoes for a savory **Tortilla de Papas (Potato Omelet)**.

Tortilla de Papas y Chorizo (Potato and Sausage Omelet)

You can also follow this same recipe for **Tortilla de Papas y Chorizo (Potato and Sausage Omelet)**. *Serves 4 | 218 calories per serving.* Fry 1/2 cup of diced potatoes in a small frying pan over medium-high heat, with 1/2 cup of oil, for about 8-10 minutes until they are golden and crispy. Add the potatoes along with 1 diced link of *chorizo* (Spanish-style sausage) instead of the plantains.

Tortilla de Papas y Chorizo (Potato and Sausage Omelet) | Pan con Bistec (Steak Sandwich) | Chuletas (Pork Chops)

Bistec (Pan-Fried Steak)

Serves 8 | 148 calories per serving | Favorite of: María Teresa Suarez (Tere), Clara Aurora Matos (Toti), María Caridad García (Cary), Marilyn Marrero, Alain Fernandez, Kevin Herrera, Natalie Caridad Fernandez (Naty), Janelle Audrey Marrero and Julianna Beatriz Marrero

Ingredients:
8 thin-cut steaks, about 3 ounces each (beef round or sirloin)
1/2 teaspoon of garlic powder
1/4 teaspoon of salt
2 tablespoons of oil, for frying (divided)
1 onion (about 2 cups), sliced into strips or diced

1. When choosing your steaks, make sure they are cut very thin.
2. Season each side of the steaks with the garlic powder and salt. *
3. Add 1 tablespoon of oil to a large frying pan over high heat.
4. Once the oil is hot, add the steaks, 1-2 at a time.
5. Quickly fry one side of the steaks until the uncooked side starts to turn slightly brown. Flip the steaks to cook on the other side.
6. Add more oil to the pan between batches, as needed.
7. Set the heat to medium-low, add the onions and let them soften and caramelize with the steak drippings.

* Garlic and salt. That's it. Just like Mima says, *"No le hace falta más nada."* (It doesn't need anything else.)

Pan con Bistec (Steak Sandwich)

¡Prueba Esto! (Try This!) Make it a **Pan con Bistec (Steak Sandwich)** with some fresh *pan cubano* (Cuban bread). Don't forget the crunchy potato sticks!

Chuletas (Pork Chops)

Serves 8 | 202 calories per serving | Favorite of: Adrian Fernandez (Boly)

Ingredients:
8 thin-cut pork chops, about 3 ounces each
1/2 teaspoon of garlic powder
1/2 teaspoon of salt
2 tablespoons of oil, for frying
1/2 onion (about 1 cup), sliced into strips or diced

1. Season each side of the pork chops with the garlic powder and salt.
2. Add the oil to a large frying pan over medium-high heat.
3. Once the oil is hot, sear the pork chops for about 3-4 minutes per side.
4. Set to medium-low heat and cook for another 10-15 minutes. Add the onions and allow them to caramelize while the pork chops finish cooking through.

Sopa de Pollo (Chicken Soup)

Serves 8 | 237 calories per serving | Favorite of: Waldo Ramón Herrera (Papito), Karina Gudiel and Janelle Audrey Marrero

Ingredients:

6 pieces of chicken (about 2 pounds)

1 tablespoon of an all-purpose seasoning (*BADIA Sazón Completa*® or *BADIA Sazón Tropical*®)

2 tablespoons of oil of choice

1 onion (about 2 cups), diced

4 garlic cloves (about 2 teaspoons), minced

10 cups of water

1-1/2 teaspoons (or 1 packet) of seasoning mix with *azafrán* (saffron), for color and flavor

2 teaspoons of salt

2 large potatoes, peeled and cubed

2 medium carrots, cut into rounds

Optional: 1 large *malanga* (taro) root, peeled and cubed; fresh lime juice (to taste)

1/2 pack of thin angel hair noodles (about 5 ounces)

1. Choose bone-in chicken drumsticks or thighs for more flavor. Sprinkle the seasoning blend on the chicken.
2. Add the oil to a large pot over medium heat.
3. Once the oil is hot, add the chicken, turning it occasionally, to let it brown evenly on all sides. Once the chicken is browned, add the onions and garlic, and sauté until the onions are soft and translucent.
4. Add the water, saffron seasoning mix and salt. Cook for another 15 minutes until it begins to simmer.
5. Set to medium-low heat, cover and cook for about 30 minutes until the chicken is fully cooked and it comes easily off the bones.
6. Pull out the chicken and cut it into bite-sized pieces before mixing it back in.
7. Meanwhile, add the potatoes, carrots and *malanga* (if desired). Cover and cook for about 20 minutes over medium heat, until the vegetables are all soft.
8. Add the noodles and lime (if desired) for about 5 minutes before serving.

¡No Me Digas! (You Don't Say!) Mima doesn't use a slow cooker, but I love mine, and you can make this soup in it. Add all the ingredients, except the noodles and lime juice. Cook on low for 6-8 hours, pull out the chicken and cut it into bite-sized pieces before mixing it back in. Add the noodles and cook for 8-10 minutes before serving.

¡Prueba Esto! (Try This!) Instead of cutting up the chicken in Step 6, you can also pan-fry it with a little oil over medium-high heat, until it's evenly browned and crispy on all sides. Finish it off with some fresh lime juice.

Sopa de Pollo (Chicken Soup) | Fricasé de Pollo (Stewed Chicken with Potatoes) | Carne con Papas (Stewed Beef with Potatoes)

Fricasé de Pollo (Stewed Chicken with Potatoes)

Serves 6 | 256 calories per serving | Favorite of: Julianna Beatriz Marrero

Ingredients:
6 pieces of chicken (about 2 pounds)
1 tablespoon of an all-purpose seasoning (*BADIA Sazón Completa®* or *BADIA Sazón Tropical®*)
2 tablespoons of oil of choice
1 onion (about 2 cups), diced
1/2 green and/or red bell pepper (about 1/2 cup), diced
4 garlic cloves (about 2 teaspoons), minced
2 cups of water
1-1/2 teaspoons (or 1 packet) of seasoning mix with *azafrán* (saffron), for color and flavor
1/2 cup of white cooking wine
4 ounces of canned tomato sauce
2 large potatoes, peeled and cubed
Optional: 2 tablespoons of sliced green olives

1. Choose bone-in chicken drumsticks or thighs for more flavor. Sprinkle the seasoning blend on the chicken.
2. Add the oil to a large pot over medium heat.
3. Once the oil is hot, add the chicken, turning it occasionally, to let it brown evenly on all sides.
4. Once the chicken is browned, add the onions, bell peppers and garlic, and sauté until the onions are soft and translucent.
5. Add the water, saffron seasoning mix, wine and tomato sauce. Stir well and bring to a boil.
6. Cover and cook for about 30 minutes.
7. Add the potatoes and olives (if desired). Cover and cook for another 20-30 minutes until the chicken is fully cooked and the potatoes are soft.

Carne con Papas (Stewed Beef with Potatoes)

¡Prueba Esto! (Try This!) You can follow this same recipe for **Carne con Papas (Stewed Beef with Potatoes).** *Serves 6 | 292 calories per serving.* Use 2 pounds of cubed beef stew meat instead of the chicken.

¡No Me Digas! (You Don't Say!) Mima doesn't use a slow cooker, but I love mine, and you can make both of these recipes in it. Add all the ingredients and cook on high for 4 hours or low for 6-8 hours.

Arroz con Pollo (Chicken and Yellow Rice)

Serves 8 | 474 calories per serving | Favorite of: Marilyn Marrero

Ingredients:

6 pieces of chicken (about 2 pounds)
1 tablespoon of an all-purpose seasoning (*BADIA Sazón Completa*® or *BADIA Sazón Tropical*®)
1/2 cup of oil of choice
1 onion (about 2 cups), diced
6 garlic cloves (about 1 tablespoon), minced
1 green and/or red bell pepper (about 1 cup), diced
2 teaspoons of salt
1-1/2 teaspoons (or 1 packet) of seasoning mix with *azafrán* (saffron), for color and flavor
4 ounces of canned tomato sauce
8 cups of water (divided)
Optional: 1/4 cup of sliced green olives
3 cups of long-grain white rice
1 cup of beer, or white cooking wine

1. Sprinkle the seasoning blend on the chicken.
2. Add the oil to an aluminum *caldero* (Dutch oven) over medium heat. Once the oil is hot, add the chicken, turning it occasionally until it browns evenly.
3. Add the onions, garlic and peppers. Sauté until the onions are translucent.
4. Add the salt, saffron seasoning mix, tomato sauce, 4 cups of water and olives (if desired) and bring to a boil over medium heat, stirring every few minutes.
5. Set to medium-low heat, cover and let the chicken cook by itself in the sauce for about 30 minutes.
6. Meanwhile, preheat the oven to 350 degrees. Wash the rice and drain it well.
7. Optional step: After the chicken is done, pull it out, let it cool, and cut it into bite-sized pieces before adding it back in.
8. Add the rice and remaining 4 cups of water. Set to medium heat and continue to cook, stirring softly from front to back, until it begins to boil again and the water is almost all absorbed.
9. Add the beer, stir well, and cover tightly with aluminum foil.
10. Transfer to the preheated oven for 30 minutes. Once you take it out of the oven, let it rest for about 10 minutes, and gently fluff before serving.

Arroz Imperial (Imperial Chicken and Yellow Rice)

¡Prueba Esto! (Try This!) You can use this recipe as a base for **Arroz Imperial (Imperial Chicken and Yellow Rice)**. *Serves 10 | 515 calories per serving.* Transfer the *arroz con pollo* to a greased rectangular baking dish. Evenly spread 3/4 cup of mayonnaise over the rice, and then top that with 2 cups of shredded mozzarella cheese. Return to the oven, uncovered, for another 15-20 minutes until the cheese melts and forms a slight crust around the edges. Let it cool slightly, and then cut into squares before serving.

Arroz con Salchichas (Rice and Vienna Sausages)

Serves 6 | 289 calories per serving | Favorite of: Janelle Audrey Marrero and Julianna Beatriz Marrero

Ingredients:

2 tablespoons of oil of choice

1/2 onion (about 1 cup), diced

1/2 green and/or red bell pepper (about 1/2 cup), diced

4 garlic cloves (about 2 teaspoons), minced

2 cups of long-grain white rice

2 cups of water

3 cans of Vienna sausages, drained and sliced

2 teaspoons of salt

1-1/2 teaspoons (or 1 packet) of seasoning mix with *azafrán* (saffron), for color and flavor

4 ounces of canned tomato sauce

Optional: 15 ounces of canned corn, drained

1. Add the oil to a frying pan over medium heat.
2. Once the oil is hot, sauté the onions, bell peppers and garlic for about 5 minutes. Remove from heat and set aside to cool.
3. Wash the rice, drain it well and add it to an electric rice cooker.
4. Add the water, Vienna sausages, salt, saffron seasoning mix, tomato sauce and corn (if desired).
5. Add the sautéed onions, bell peppers and garlic and stir well.
6. Cover and switch to "cook." Once the rice cooker is done, let it rest for about 15 minutes and gently fluff before serving.

Arroz Imperial (Imperial Chicken and Yellow Rice) | Arroz con Salchichas (Rice and Vienna Sausages) | Arroz con Chorizo y Garbanzos (Rice with Sausage and Chickpeas)

Arroz con Chorizo y Garbanzos (Rice with Sausage and Chickpeas)

¡Prueba Esto! (Try This!) You can follow this same recipe for **Arroz con Chorizo y Garbanzos (Rice with Sausage and Chickpeas).** *Serves 6 | 354 calories per serving.* Replace the Vienna sausages with 3 diced links of *chorizo* (Spanish-style sausage) and replace the corn with a 15-ounce can of chickpeas (drained).

Croquetas (Croquettes)

Serves 8 | 482 calories per serving | Favorite of: María Teresa Suarez (Tere)

Ingredients (Filling):
8 ounces of cooked, diced ham
1/4 cup of butter, cut into 4 pieces
3/4 cup of 2% milk
1 cup of flour
1/2 teaspoon of salt
1/2 teaspoon of garlic powder
1/4 teaspoon of black pepper
1/4 teaspoon of onion powder
1/4 teaspoon of dried oregano
1 teaspoon of dried parsley flakes
1 teaspoon of white cooking wine

Ingredients (Breading):
2 large eggs
2 cups of *galleta molida* (cracker meal), or 1 sleeve of finely ground saltine crackers
1-1/2 cups of oil, for frying

1. Use a food processor to grind the ham and set it aside.
2. Add the butter to a large frying pan over medium heat.
3. Once the butter is melted and sizzling, add the milk and heat thoroughly.
4. Mix in the flour, salt, garlic, pepper, onion, oregano, parsley and wine.
5. Add the ham, mix into a dough-like consistency, and cook for 5 minutes.
6. Transfer to a bowl and refrigerate for 1-2 hours until it hardens a bit.
7. Shape the dough into 18-20 thick cylinders.
8. Optional step: Refrigerate the *croquetas* for 30 minutes on a baking sheet. This will make it easier to bread them later.
9. Beat the eggs in a shallow bowl, and add the cracker meal to another bowl.
10. Dip each *croqueta* in the egg, and then the cracker meal. (Optional: for a little more crunch, repeat this step so each *croqueta* is breaded two times.)
11. Add the oil to a deep pot over medium heat. Once the oil is hot, fry the *croquetas* in a single layer, turning frequently until golden all around.

¡Prueba Esto! (Try This!) You can make *croquetas* with various fillings. Try it with beef, chicken, or salmon.

Croquetas (Croquettes) | Frijoles Negros (Black Beans) | Mima's "Famous" Congrí (Rice and Black Beans)

Frijoles Negros (Black Beans)

Serves 12 | 124 calories per serving | Favorite of: Clara Aurora Matos (Toti), Kevin Herrera, Julianna Beatriz Marrero, Emma Grace Gudiel and Anna Carolina Gudiel (Annie)

16-ounce pack of dry black beans
10 cups of water
1/4 cup of oil of choice
1 onion (about 2 cups), diced
4 garlic cloves (about 2 teaspoons), minced
1/2 green bell pepper (about 1/2 cup), diced
1 bay leaf
2 teaspoons of salt
2 teaspoons of an all-purpose seasoning (*BADIA Sazón Completa*® or *BADIA Sazón Tropical*®)
1 teaspoon of olive oil
1 teaspoon of white vinegar

1. Wash the beans well and pick out any stones. Add the beans and water to a large pot and bring to a boil over high heat.
2. Set to medium-low heat, cover and cook for 1 to 1-1/2 hours. *
3. Add the oil to a large frying pan over medium heat. Once the oil is hot, add the onions, garlic and green bell peppers. Sauté over medium heat until the onions are soft and translucent. Add the mixture to the beans.
4. Add the bay leaf, salt and seasoning blend. Stir well, cover and keep cooking over low heat for 15 minutes.
5. Remove the bay leaf. Stir in the olive oil and vinegar right before serving.

* Just like Mima says, "*Mientas más suave, más rico.*" (The softer they are, the better they will taste.)

Mima's "Famous" Congrí (Rice and Black Beans)

Serves 16 * | 205 calories per serving | Favorite of: María Teresa Suarez (Tere), Clara Aurora Matos (Toti), María Caridad García (Cary), Marilyn Marrero, Karina Gudiel, Emmanuel Matos (Manny), Alain Fernandez, Adrian Fernandez (Boly), Daniel Matos (Danny) and Maggie Cruz ("Baby" Maggie)

Ingredients:
16-ounce pack of dry black beans
10 cups of water
1/2 cup of oil of choice, plus 2 tablespoons (divided)
1 onion (about 2 cups), diced
8 garlic cloves (about 4 teaspoons), minced
1 green bell pepper (about 1 cup), diced
4 cups of long-grain white rice
2 bay leaves
2 tablespoons of an all-purpose seasoning (*BADIA Sazón Completa*® or *BADIA Sazón Tropical*®)
4 teaspoons of salt

(Recipe continued on next page.)

1. Wash the beans well and pick out any stones. Add the beans and water to a large pot and bring just to a boil over medium-high heat.
2. Set to medium-low heat, cover and let the beans cook for about 40 minutes until they are soft, but still firm and whole.
3. Add 1/2 cup of oil to an aluminum *caldero* (Dutch oven) over medium heat. Sauté the onions, garlic and peppers until the onions are soft and translucent.
4. Preheat the oven to 350 degrees. Wash the rice, drain it well and set it aside.
5. Strain the beans and add them to the *caldero*. Do not discard the tinted water.
6. Add 6 cups of the tinted water to the *caldero*.
7. Add the rice, bay leaves, seasoning blend and salt. Bring to a boil over medium-high heat. Stir gently and cook until the water is almost all absorbed.
8. Cover tightly with aluminum foil and transfer to the preheated oven for 30 minutes. Once you take it out of the oven, let it rest for about 10 minutes.
9. Spread the remaining 2 tablespoons of the oil evenly over the top of the *congrí*. Gently fluff and remove the bay leaves before serving.

* This is by far the most requested dish from Mima's kitchen. It's hard to remember a Christmas, church pot-luck or large family gathering without Mima's "famous" *congrí*. This recipe makes a lot, because that's how Mima always makes it... enough to feed everyone who shows up. If there are leftovers, it's even better the next day!

Tostones (Twice-Fried Green Plantains)

Serves 6 | 227 calories per serving

Ingredients:
2 green plantains
Oil, for frying
Salt, to taste

1. Peel and cut the plantains into rounds, about 2-inches thick.
2. Cover about 1/3 of a frying pan with oil, enough for the bottom half of the plantains to be covered while frying, and set to medium heat.
3. Once the oil is hot, carefully add the plantain rounds in a single layer.
4. When they start to turn golden, flip them to cook on the other side.
5. Place the plantains on a paper towel to drain and cool slightly.
6. Use a *tostonera* (plantain press) or paper towel to flatten the plantains.
7. Fry the flattened plantains over medium-high heat for about 1 minute on each side, until they are golden and crispy. Sprinkle with salt before serving.

Tostones (Twice-Fried Green Plantains) | Chicharritas (Green Plantain Chips) | Sopa de Plátano (Creamy Plantain Soup)

Chicharritas (Green Plantain Chips)

Serves 8 | 170 calories per serving

Ingredients:

2 green plantains

Oil, for frying

Salt, to taste

1. Peel and cut the plantains into very thin, round chips.
2. Cover about 1/3 of a frying pan with oil and set to medium heat.
3. Once the oil is hot, carefully add the plantains in batches.
4. Fry the plantains over medium heat for 2-3 minutes, carefully turning them often, until they are golden and crispy. Sprinkle with salt before serving.

Sopa de Plátano (Creamy Plantain Soup)

Serves 2 | 210 calories per serving

Ingredients:

1 teaspoon of oil of choice

1/4 onion (about 1/2 cup), diced

1 garlic clove (about 1/2 teaspoon), minced

2-1/2 cups of water

1 chicken flavor bouillon tablet, crushed

1/2 teaspoon of salt

1/4 teaspoon of black pepper

1 green plantain

Oil, for frying

1. Add 1 teaspoon of oil to a large pot over medium heat.
2. Add the onions and garlic, and sauté until the onions are soft and translucent.
3. Add the water, bouillon tablet, salt and pepper, and stir well. Cook for about 15 minutes over medium heat.
4. Meanwhile, peel and cut the plantains into very thin, round chips.
5. Cover about 1/3 of a frying pan with oil and set to medium heat.
6. Once the oil is hot, carefully add the plantains in batches.
7. Fry the plantains over medium heat for 2-3 minutes, carefully turning them often, until they are golden and crispy. Place the plantains on a paper towel to help absorb some of the excess oil while you finish cooking the rest.
8. Carefully add 1-1/2 cups of the broth mixture to a blender, along with the chips. Puree until smooth, adding more of the broth mixture as needed, until it reaches your desired consistency.

¡No Me Digas! (You Don't Say!) For a shortcut, you can skip Steps 4-7 and use 1-1/2 cups of store-bought *chicharritas* or *mariquitas* (another name for green plantain chips, usually cut into long strips).

Boniato Acaramelado (Caramelized White Sweet Potato)

Serves 4 | 150 calories per serving

Ingredients:

2 *boniatos* (white sweet potatoes)
1 teaspoon of salt
2 tablespoons of butter
1/4 cup of granulated sugar

1. Wash and carefully peel the sweet potatoes.
2. Fill a large pot with water, add the whole sweet potatoes and salt, and bring to a boil over medium-high heat.
3. Lower to medium heat and let them cook for about 20 minutes, until they are soft enough to pierce with a fork.
4. Drain and let them cool slightly before carefully cutting them into thick rounds, about 1-inch each.
5. Add the butter to a large frying pan over medium heat.
6. Once the butter is melted and sizzling, add the sweet potato slices.
7. Gradually sprinkle with sugar as you turn the pieces a few times every 1-2 minutes, to let them evenly caramelize on all sides.

Boniato Frito (White Sweet Potato Fries)

Serves 4 | 194 calories per serving

Ingredients:

2 *boniatos* (white sweet potatoes)
Oil, for frying
2 tablespoons of granulated sugar

1. Wash and peel the sweet potatoes, and then cut them into thin wedges.
2. Cover about 1/3 of a frying pan with oil, enough for the sweet potatoes to be fully covered while frying, and set to medium heat.
3. Once the oil is hot, carefully add the wedges and fry them for 8-10 minutes, carefully turning them often until they are golden all around and fully cooked through. Sprinkle the sugar over the fries right before serving.

Boniato Acaramelado (Caramelized White Sweet Potato) | Yuca con Mojo (Cassava with Citrus-Garlic Sauce) | Yuca Frita (Cassava Fries)

Yuca con Mojo (Cassava with Citrus-Garlic Sauce)

Serves 8 | 275 calories per serving

Ingredients (Cassava):
2 pounds of *yuca* (cassava), fresh or frozen
2 teaspoons of salt

Ingredients (Sauce):
1/4 cup of olive oil
1/2 onion (about 1 cup), sliced into strips
12 cloves of garlic (about 2 tablespoons), minced
Juice of 1/2 *naranja agria* (bitter orange) or 1 lime (about 2 tablespoons)
Salt and black pepper, to taste

1. Fill a large pot with water and place it over high heat.
2. Add the cassava to the pot. Note: If using fresh cassava, make sure to peel the skin first and chop it into thick, 3-4 inch pieces.
3. Bring to a boil, lower to medium-high heat, and let it cook for 20 minutes.
4. Drain and discard the water. Fill the pot with fresh water.
5. Add the salt, and bring to a boil over medium-high heat once again, for about 10-15 minutes.
6. Once the cassava pieces start to split open in the center, remove from heat. Leave the cassava in the pot of hot water until ready to serve.
7. Meanwhile, prepare the sauce. Add the olive oil to a frying pan over medium heat. Add the onions and garlic and sauté over medium heat until the onions are soft and translucent. Do not let the onions brown or they will turn bitter. Add the orange juice, salt and pepper, and cook for another 3-5 minutes.
8. Drain the cassava and cut each piece in half. Remove the hard, stem-like piece in the center of each chunk.
9. Place the cassava on a large platter and pour the sauce over it right before serving.

Yuca Frita (Cassava Fries)

¡Prueba Esto! (Try This!) *Serves 10 | 371 calories per serving.* To make **Yuca Frita (Cassava Fries)**, follow Steps 1-4, and after draining the cassava, cut the pieces into thick wedges. Be sure to remove the hard, stem-like piece in the center of each chunk. Fry the wedges in about 1-1/2 cup of oil over medium-high heat for about 5 minutes, until they are golden brown. Sprinkle with salt before serving. Optional step: Follow the instructions in Step 7 to make the sauce for dipping, using finely diced onions.

Frijoles Colorados (Red Kidney Beans)

Serves 12 | 173 calories per serving

16-ounce pack of red kidney beans
10 cups of water
1/4 cup of oil of choice
1 onion (about 2 cups), diced
4 garlic cloves (about 2 teaspoons), minced
1/2 green bell pepper (about 1/2 cup), diced
Optional: 1/2 cup of diced pre-cooked ham, bacon or pork chops
2 teaspoons of salt
1-1/2 teaspoons (or 1 packet) of seasoning mix with *azafrán* (saffron), for color and flavor
1/4 cup of canned tomato sauce
1 medium potato, peeled and diced

1. Wash the beans well and pick out any stones. Add the beans and water to a large pot and bring to a boil over high heat.
2. Set to medium-low heat, cover and let the beans cook for about 1 to 1-1/2 hours until they are very soft.
3. Add the oil to a large frying pan over medium heat. Once the oil is hot, add the onions, garlic, green bell peppers and ham (if desired). Sauté over medium heat until the onions are soft and translucent. Add the mixture to the pot of beans.
4. Add the salt, seasoning blend, saffron seasoning, tomato sauce and potatoes.
5. Stir well, cover and keep cooking over low heat for about 20 minutes, until the potatoes are soft.

Frijoles Colorados (Red Kidney Beans) | Pollo Salteado (Stir-Fried Chicken) | Picadillo (Sautéed Ground Beef)

Bistec Salteado (Stir-Fried Steak)

Serves 8 | 160 calories per serving

Ingredients:
8 thin-cut steaks, about 3 ounces each (beef round or sirloin), cut into strips
2 teaspoons of an all-purpose seasoning (*BADIA Sazón Completa*® or *BADIA Sazón Tropical*®)
2 tablespoons of oil, for frying
4 cups of onions and green and/or red bell peppers, sliced into strips
Optional: 2 tablespoons of soy sauce or white wine

1. Sprinkle the seasoning blend on the steak.
2. Add the oil to a large frying pan over medium-high heat.
3. Once the oil is hot, add the steak and stir-fry it until it's evenly browned.
4. Add the onions and peppers, along with the soy sauce or white wine (if desired) to the pan.
5. Reduce the heat to medium-low. Let the onions and peppers cook with the steak for about 10 minutes, until they soften and caramelize with the steak drippings.

Pollo Salteado (Stir-Fried Chicken)

¡Prueba Esto! (Try This!) You can use 1 pound of boneless chicken breast and follow this same recipe for **Pollo Salteado (Stir-Fried Chicken)**. *Serves 4 | 225 calories per serving.*

Picadillo (Sautéed Ground Beef)

Serves 4 | 438 calories per serving

Ingredients:
2 tablespoons of oil of choice
1 pound of lean ground beef
2 teaspoons of an all-purpose seasoning (*BADIA Sazón Completa®* or *BADIA Sazón Tropical®*)
1/2 onion (about 1 cup), diced
2 cloves of garlic (about 1 teaspoon), minced
4 ounces of canned tomato sauce
1/4 cup of white cooking wine
1/2 cup of water
Optional add-ins: 1/4 cup of sliced green olives, 1/4 cup of raisins, 1/2 cup of diced potatoes

1. Add the oil to a large frying pan over medium heat.
2. Once the oil is hot, add the ground beef, seasoning blend, onions and garlic.
3. Brown the meat, breaking up any large chunks as it cooks.
4. Add the tomato sauce, wine, water and any optional add-ins, except the potatoes.
5. Set to low heat and let it simmer for about 15 minutes.
6. Optional step: Meanwhile, fry the potatoes (if desired) in a small frying pan over medium-high heat, with 1/2 cup of oil, for about 8-10 minutes. Mix in the crispy potatoes right before serving.

Ropa Vieja (Sautéed Shredded Beef)

Serves 4 | 382 calories per serving

Ingredients:

2 teaspoons of an all-purpose seasoning (*BADIA Sazón Completa*® or *BADIA Sazón Tropical*®)

2 tablespoons of oil of choice

1-1/2 pounds of flank steak

4 cloves of garlic (about 2 teaspoons), minced

8 ounces of canned tomato sauce

1/4 cup of white cooking wine

1/2 cup of water

2 cups of onions and green and/or red bell peppers, sliced into strips

1. Sprinkle the seasoning blend all around the flank steak.
2. Add the oil to a large pot over medium heat and sear both sides of the steak.
3. Add the garlic, tomato sauce, wine and water. Let it come to a simmer, cover and cook for 1 hour over medium-low heat.
4. Pull out the steak, let it cool slightly, and shred it using two forks.
5. Return to the pot, add in the onions and bell peppers, stir well, and cook for another 30 minutes over low heat.

¡No Me Digas! (You Don't Say!) Mima doesn't use a slow cooker, but I love mine, and you can make this dish in it. Add all the ingredients, except for the onions and peppers, and cook on low for 6-8 hours. Shred the beef, add the onions and peppers, and cook for another 30 minutes.

Ropa Vieja (Sautéed Shredded Beef) | Pollo Asado (Oven-Roasted Chicken) | Boliche / Carne Asada (Beef Pot Roast)

Pollo Asado (Oven-Roasted Chicken)

Serves 6 | 392 calories per serving

Ingredients:

Whole chicken (approximately 4 pounds)

Juice of 1 *naranja agria* (bitter orange) or 2 limes (about 1/4 cup)

6 cloves of garlic (about 1 tablespoon), minced

1 tablespoon of salt

1 tablespoon of an all-purpose seasoning (*BADIA Sazón Completa*® or *BADIA Sazón Tropical*®)

3 large potatoes, peeled and cubed

1. If you have time the night before, follow Steps 2 and 3 and let the chicken marinate overnight in the refrigerator. If not, start with Step 2 now.
2. Cut the chicken in half along the backbone, remove the neck bone and giblets, wash it well and pat it dry with paper towels.
3. Add the orange juice, garlic, salt and seasoning blend to the chicken.
4. Preheat the oven to 350 degrees. Lightly grease the bottom of a covered roasting pan.
5. Place the chicken, breast down, in the roasting pan. Cover and bake in the preheated oven for 1 hour.
6. Turn the chicken, breast up, and add the potatoes all around the edges.
7. Return the covered pan to the oven for another 30-40 minutes until the chicken is fully cooked through and the potatoes are soft.
8. Remove the cover and return to the oven for 10 minutes to let it brown.

Boliche / Carne Asada (Beef Pot Roast)

Serves 8 | 439 calories per serving

Ingredients:
Eye round roast (approximately 3 pounds)
Juice of 1/2 *naranja agria* (bitter orange) or 1 lime (about 2 tablespoons)
1 cup of white cooking wine
6 cloves of garlic (about 1 tablespoon), minced
1 teaspoon of salt
2 teaspoons of an all-purpose seasoning (*BADIA Sazón Completa®* or *BADIA Sazón Tropical®*)
2 tablespoons of oil of choice
2 large potatoes, peeled and cubed

1. If you have time the night before, follow Step 2 and let the roast marinate overnight in the refrigerator. If not, start with Step 2 now.
2. Add the orange juice, wine, garlic, salt and seasoning blend to the roast.
3. Preheat the oven to 350 degrees. Lightly grease the bottom of a covered roasting pan with the oil.
4. Place the roast in the pan, fatty side up. Cover and bake it in the preheated oven for 1-1/2 hours. Remove from the oven and let it cool slightly.
5. Carefully slice the roast into rounds, about 1-inch thick. Arrange the pieces on the bottom of the pan, and add the potatoes. Use a large spoon to scoop some of the drippings from the pan over the meat and potatoes.
6. Return the covered pan to the oven for another 30 minutes until the meat and potatoes are fully cooked through.

¡No Me Digas! (You Don't Say!) Mima doesn't use a slow cooker, but I love mine, and you can make this roast in it. Grease the bottom of the slow cooker with the oil, place the potatoes on the bottom, and the roast on top of the potatoes, fatty side up. Add the orange juice, wine, garlic, salt and seasoning blend. Cook on low for 6-8 hours. Carefully slice the roast, and place it back into the slow cooker for another 30 minutes.

Paleta de Puerco Asada (Oven-Roasted Pork Shoulder)

Serves 10 | 365 calories per serving

Ingredients:

4-pound boneless pork shoulder roast

Juice of 1 *naranja agria* (bitter orange) or 2 limes (about 4 tablespoons)

6 cloves of garlic (about 1 tablespoon), minced

2 teaspoons of salt

1 tablespoon of an all-purpose seasoning (*BADIA Sazón Completa®* or *BADIA Sazón Tropical®*)

2 tablespoons of oil of choice

1. The most important step is to let the pork marinate overnight. Carefully pierce the pork a few times on each side with the sharp end of a knife. Rub the pork with the orange juice and add the garlic, salt and seasoning blend. Place it in a sealed container in the refrigerator.
2. Preheat the oven to 350 degrees. Lightly grease the bottom of a covered roasting pan with the oil.
3. Place the pork in the roasting pan, fatty side up, and pour the excess marinade into the pan.
4. Cover and bake the pork in the preheated oven for 1-1/2 hours.
5. Turn the pork over, cover and return to the oven for about 1 more hour, until it's cooked all the way through and starting to brown.
6. Shred the pork, removing some of the excess fat. Return the shredded meat to the oven for another 15 minutes, uncovered, to let it brown and absorb some of the flavor from the drippings.

Pan con Lechón (Cuban Pulled Pork Sandwich)

Make it a **Pan con Lechón (Cuban Pulled Pork Sandwich)** with some fresh *pan cubano* (Cuban bread). Optional: sauté some onions and garlic with a little olive oil for about 5 minutes, and drizzle it all over the sandwich before serving.

Paleta de Puerco Asada (Oven-Roasted Pork Shoulder) | Pechuga de Pavo Asada (Roasted Turkey Breast).| Harina de Maíz (Savory Cornmeal)

Pechuga de Pavo Asada (Roasted Turkey Breast)

¡Prueba Esto! (Try This!) You can slightly adjust the pork shoulder recipe to make **Pechuga de Pavo Asada (Roasted Turkey Breast).** *Serves 8 | 328 calories per serving.* Replace the pork with a 3-pound boneless turkey breast (do not remove the netting). Skip the salt if it is pre-brined with salt. Rub 4 tablespoons of softened butter over the top of the breast in Step 3. Reduce the cooking time to 1 hour, without flipping it. Let it cool slightly, remove the netting and slice the meat. Cover the pan and return it to the oven for another 30 minutes. Beware: You may never want to go back to a traditional Thanksgiving turkey!

¡No Me Digas! (You Don't Say!) Mima doesn't use a slow cooker, but I love mine, and you can make the pork shoulder and turkey breast in it. Add all the ingredients and cook on low for 6-8 hours (pork) or 4-6 hours (turkey). Shred or slice the meat, removing some of the excess fat as needed, and place it back into the slow cooker. Remove some of the excess liquid from the slow cooker as needed, and cook for another 30 minutes. You can also drizzle some of the liquid over the shredded/sliced meat and put it in the oven for 15-20 minutes at 400 degrees to give it a little crisp around the edges.

Harina de Maíz (Savory Cornmeal)

Serves 8 | 141 calories per serving

Ingredients:
8 cups of water
2 cups of fine yellow cornmeal
2 teaspoons of salt
1/2 teaspoon of black pepper
2 tablespoons of oil of choice

1. Add the water to a large pot over medium-low heat.
2. Meanwhile, pour the cornmeal into a large bowl. Wash the cornmeal with cold water to remove the excess starch. Let it settle for about a minute, and then drain it carefully.
3. Add the cornmeal to the pot, along with the salt, pepper and oil.
4. Stir continuously while it cooks for about 15-20 minutes, until it begins to thicken and the water is almost all absorbed.
5. Reduce to low heat and continue cooking, while stirring, until it reaches the consistency of creamy grits or polenta, about 15-20 minutes.
6. Try serving it with *huevos fritos* (fried eggs), or with flavorful meats like *picadillo* (sautéed ground beef) or *paleta de puerco asada* (oven-roasted pork shoulder).

Harina Dulce de Maíz (Sweet Cornmeal Pudding)

Serves 12 | 364 calories per serving

Ingredients:
8 cups of water
2 cups of fine yellow cornmeal
1 teaspoon of salt
2 cinnamon sticks
12 ounces of canned evaporated milk
14 ounces of canned sweetened condensed milk
1 cup of sugar
1/4 cup of butter, cut into 4 pieces
Ground cinnamon, to taste

1. Add the water to a large pot over medium-low heat.
2. Meanwhile, pour the cornmeal into a large bowl. Wash the cornmeal with cold water to remove the excess starch. Let it settle for about a minute, and then drain it carefully.
3. Add the cornmeal to the pot, along with the salt and cinnamon sticks.
4. Stir continuously while it cooks for about 15-20 minutes, until it begins to thicken and the water is almost all absorbed.
5. Remove the cinnamon stick and add the evaporated and condensed milk, sugar and butter.
6. Reduce to low heat and continue cooking for about 20 minutes, while stirring, until it thickens to a pudding or applesauce consistency. Keep in mind that it will continue to thicken while cooling.
7. Sprinkle with ground cinnamon just before serving while still warm. Any leftovers can be refrigerated and heated with a splash of milk.

Arroz con Leche (Rice Pudding)

Serves 12 | 249 calories per serving

Ingredients:
12-ounce pack of short-grain white rice (*Valencia* style)
4 cups of water
1 cinnamon stick
1 orange peel
1/2 teaspoon of salt
2 tablespoons of sugar
12 ounces of canned evaporated milk
14 ounces of canned sweetened condensed milk
12 ounces of 2% milk
Ground cinnamon, to taste

1. Wash the rice and drain it well.
2. Add the rice, water, cinnamon stick and orange peel to a large pot over medium-high heat and let it come to a boil.
3. Lower to medium heat and stir continuously while it cooks for about 15 minutes, until the rice begins to soften and the water is almost all absorbed.
4. Remove the cinnamon stick and orange peel.
5. Stir in the salt, sugar, evaporated and condensed milk, and the regular milk.
6. Let it continue to cook over low heat, making sure to stir continuously so it doesn't stick, for about 10 minutes or to your desired consistency. Keep in mind that it will continue to thicken while cooling.
7. Pour into small bowls, sprinkle with ground cinnamon, and chill in the refrigerator before serving.

Harina Dulce de Maíz (Sweet Cornmeal Pudding) | Arroz con Leche (Rice Pudding) | Mermelada de Mango (Mango Jam)

Mermelada de Mango (Mango Jam)

Serves 8 | 148 calories per serving

Ingredients:
2 large extra ripe mangoes, peeled and cubed (about 4 cups)
1 cup of granulated sugar

1. The most important step is to wait until the mangoes are ripe and sweet.
2. Add the mango cubes to a blender and puree until smooth.
3. Pour into a large pot over medium-low heat, add the sugar, and stir well.
4. Stir every couple of minutes while it cooks, for about 15 minutes, until it thickens to a jam-like consistency.
5. Pour into small containers and chill in the refrigerator. Enjoy with toast or saltine crackers, as an ice-cream topping, or with a few slices of cream cheese for a sweet-and-salty treat.

Jugo de Mango (Mango Juice)

Serves 2 | 202 calories per serving

Ingredients:
1 large ripe mango, peeled and cubed (about 2 cups)
2 cups of water
1/4 cup of granulated sugar
1-1/2 cups of ice

1. Add the mango, water and sugar to a blender and puree.
2. Add the ice, puree until smooth, and serve immediately.

Batido de Mango (Mango Shake)

Serves 2 | 240 calories per serving

Ingredients:
2 cups of ripe mango, peeled and cubed (fresh or frozen)
1-1/4 cup of 2% milk
2 tablespoons of granulated sugar
1 cup of ice

1. Add the mango, milk and sugar to a blender and puree.
2. Add the ice, puree until smooth, and serve immediately.

Batido de Mamey (Mamey Shake)

¡Prueba Esto! (Try This!) You can follow this same recipe for **Batido de Mamey (Mamey Shake).** *Serves 2 | 328 calories per serving.* Replace the mango with fresh or frozen mamey.

Batido de Trigo (Wheat Shake)

You can also follow this recipe for **Batido de Trigo (Wheat Shake).** *Serves 2 | 291 calories per serving.* Replace the mango with puffed wheat cereal and add 1 more tablespoon of sugar.

Batido de Mango (Mango Shake) | Batido de Mamey (Mamey Shake) | Batido de Trigo (Wheat Shake)

Join our Familión:

Join us as we celebrate all that we've learned from Mima and seek to carry on her legacy through our hearts, traditions and kitchens.

We would love to hear about your favorite dishes from the book. Don't forget to tag us in your pics!

Instagram | Facebook: @justlikemimas

Web: justlikemimas.com

Email: justlikemimas@gmail.com

¡Buen Provecho! (Enjoy!)

Acknowledgements:

I thank God for his faithfulness. Every good thing in my life is a reminder of his mercy and grace. I also want to express my love and gratitude to:

Mima. A few years ago, I ran across an article that explained that women develop all their eggs while growing within their own mothers' wombs. This means the microscopic egg cells that would eventually become *me* started inside *you* when you were pregnant with my mom. What a beautiful connection! I am immensely thankful for your influence in my life, and I love you more than the simple words in this book could ever express.

My husband, Jonathan. Thank you for your love, humor, and constant support (from emotional support to tech support and everything in between). Thank you for reminding me that there is time for everything, for letting me dream, and for sometimes dreaming bigger than me. I could not have done this without you! My girls, Janelle and Julianna. Your excitement for this project made me even more certain it was worth it. Thank you for all your help and for cheering me on from start to finish. Because of you, it turned out even more beautifully than I imagined.

My mom. Thank you for answering my (often prying) questions, gathering photos, and helping me confirm countless dates and details. Thank you for being a wonderful "Mami" to Karina and me, an amazing "Yeya" to our girls, and for your constant encouragement and love. My sister, Karina. Thank you for capturing these beautiful pictures of Mima, and for always being there for me. You are the best sister and the best "Titi" to my girls. Let's keep these family traditions going!

Pipo, Toti, Cary, Papito and the rest of our *Familión*. Thank you for sharing your stories and photos to honor Mima and preserve these memories for our future generations. Being a part of this family is one of the greatest blessings in my life.

All the influential friends, teachers and mentors who have inspired me to write over the years. From Cherie Branning (who will always be Mrs. Shepard to me) at Miami Southridge High School, to my professors at Florida International University, to all the colleagues who've helped me grow along the way. I'm especially thankful for Danny Franks and Carolyn Wilson, my friends and partners in ministry at The Summit Church, who read my early drafts and provided great feedback and encouragement. And for Chris Pappalardo, whose insight was invaluable, and whose Writing Cohort gave me the push I needed to "just write, already!" (right before the quarantine began).

And speaking of the quarantine... Thanks, 2020. While I am very empathetic to the pain and loss that many have experienced as a result of the COVID-19 pandemic, this season has allowed me to take something that was only a faint idea into a tangible reality.

Cruz María Herrera (Mima) and Marilyn Marrero in Naples, Florida – June 2020.

Recipe Index: